MW00448329

BIG DATA IN REAL ESTATE
BE A MILLIONAIRE

Authors

Patrick C. O'Connor

Michael L. Miller

Mark Verrett

ABOUT THE AUTHORS

Patrick O'Connor, MAI, president of Enriched Data and O'Connor & Associates is an entrepreneur and innovator whose "Big Data" technology is poised to change how professionals do business across the United States. Pat started O'Connor & Associates in 1974 and since that time it has grown to be the largest independent real estate research and appraisal services firm in the Southwest.

Pat has over thirty years of experience in appraising commercial real estate properties, property tax reduction and federal tax reduction. He is a graduate of University of Houston and Harvard Business School with a Master of Business Administration.

Pat O'Connor's first book, *Cut Your Property Taxes*, is a book that empowers individuals to challenge the appraisal district to reduce assessed property value. He has been interviewed on many syndicated radio and television programs including *CNN, Fox News*, and *CNBC*. He has been featured in publications including *Globe St, Monthly Finance Magazine, Mortgage Compliance Magazine, Wall Street Journal, New York Times, USA Today, National Real Estate Investor, Houston Chronicle, Houston Business Journal, The Appraisal Journal*, and the National Apartment Association's *UNITS* magazine. If you wish to get in touch with Pat, email him at poconnor@poconnor.com.

Michael Miller, MAI, has been an appraiser and consultant in real estate for over 25 years. He is a leader in Real Estate's transformation through "Big Data" technology. Michael is the Executive Managing Director of Enriched Data, the largest enriched real estate database in the United States. Previously a Senior Managing Director who helped start Grubb & Ellis Landauer Valuation Advisory Services appraisal platform; Senior Director, with Cushman & Wakefield of Arizona and Texas for 17 years and with CB Commercial Real Estate Group, Inc. (CBRE) as an Assistant Vice President for 8 years.

As an MAI designated member of the Appraisal Institute, the long history of evaluating individual and portfolio real estate properties has allowed the Sage Group to build on the 20 year foundation of information O'Connor & Associates has built. Michael's passion is bringing together "best in class" local businesses with premier real estate and information data under proprietary technology. To get in touch with Michael, email him at mmiller@enricheddata.com.

Mark E. Verrett, SRA, Managing Director of Enriched Data, is a second-generation appraiser with 17 years in the real estate industry. Mark began his career by using technology and Big Data to fuel exponential growth in his residential valuation business. Using this success as a springboard, Mark became a leader in Big Data and cloud-based technologies within the real estate arena. Along with partnering applications, he has worked to build a national real estate database in an effort to get data in the hands of real estate professionals and the public. Mark's work has proven that when technology and Big Data are properly applied to real estate, they can revolutionize the industry by significantly increasing productivity and improving work quality through depth of analysis. From automated valuations to mortgage backed securities, Mark is leading the way in innovative uses of Big Data to meet the needs of major industry.

Mark graduated Summa Cum Laude from St. Edwards University with a BS degree, and later earned a MS degree in Real Estate Finance from Texas A&M University. He has been recognized by the Appraisal Institute as "the next generation of appraisal leaders." He currently serves as an officer of the Houston Chapter of the Appraisal Institute, previously served as National Chairman of the Leadership Development and Advisory Council, and is continually active in local, state, and national AI activities. If you wish to get in touch with Mark, he can be reached via email at mark@enricheddata.com.

Visit www.BigDataMillionaire.com for more information on the authors and upcoming appearances.

PROLOGUE

Big Data – it is here to stay, and will change the way we live, work and play. The processing of Big Data will help determine who to marry, where to live, where to retire, and what employment opportunities are available. Figuring out ways to use big data will allow you and your company to be proficient. Big Data will allow comparisons like never before, like where to live if you want to live the longest. Recreational enthusiasts can quickly evaluate work and home locations that best fit their lifestyles. Health-conscious families are always exploring evolving lifestyles and healthy living options. In addition, any one of these buyer segments can drive a market's appreciation, a leading factor for wealth creation for U.S. families.

The real estate buzzword is "**Big Data**." Wikipedia defines **Big Data** as a collection of data sets so large and complex that they are difficult to process using on-hand database management tools or traditional data processing applications. The big data processing challenges include capturing, curation, storage, searching, sharing, transferring, analysis, and visualization.

Larger data sets are possible due to the assemblage of single sets of related data that can be supplemented with additional relative information allowing correlations to "spot trends." The result is larger aggregate data collections that are meaningful if properly filtered and processed.

Companies that process Big Data in real estate can trade for over 100x in earnings, elite pricing previously only reserved for technology stocks. Moreover, what historically took a building full of servers is now executed on a hosted website with intense security protocols for a few thousand dollars per month. Intranet connections between companies can transfer millions of records across the world in split seconds. Watches and handheld devices milliliters thick access data that now only cost a few hundred dollars. Some of the largest companies in the world provide apps for these devices often for free, or for a few cents per application. The technology world has changed, and in the future, it will change even faster.

You can now:

1. Isolate the data that is important to you; and

2. Interpret that data in a meaningful way to make you more productive and earn more money!

An Internet search retrieves millions of results, but this random knowledge does not help your cause. Isolating factors that are important to you is the key to gaining "laser focus" and obtaining the knowledge that allows you to be "best in class." For example successful home investors focus on a zip code or a neighborhood where they know every house and stay updated daily and weekly on what is happening in the market, not just by searching the Internet, but also by driving and walking the streets of the areas where they want to invest. Investors not only search the Multiple Listing Service, but also research foreclosures, tax auctions, go to homeowner association meetings and community outings. Finding the anomalies or the outliers in a market is the key to effective investing. Investors know that money is made on the "buy side."

While the mind is an incredible processor, interpreting data via spreadsheets or databases is key to seeing what is happening today and comparing that information to the past. An Excel spreadsheet is a simple form of documentation. Processing potential leads and acquisitions through Smart Sheets, Sales Force, Goldkey, Act, Outlook, etc. is better than simple documentation. When analyzing multiple properties or units, Rent Manager, Asset Dynamics, SimplifyEm, Argus, and others can provide meaningful lease-by-lease analysis for sophisticated investment properties for investors. Imagine what you could do if you tracked all home sales and listings in the neighborhood where you were born since you were born. The historical knowledge would allow you to be a good judge of the future.

Volume of Data Doubling Every Two Years

Moore's Law, named after Gordon Moore, one of the founders of Intel, estimated that the power of semiconductor chips would double every two years. The same is now occurring with data due to a change in the number of devices that measure and transmit it. O'Connor's Law states, "the volume of data available will double every two years." The following is a list of volume of content on the web.

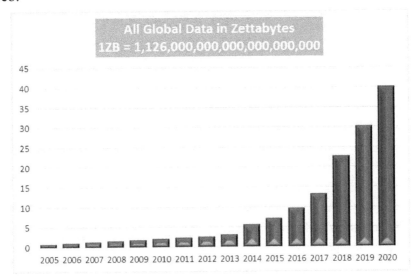

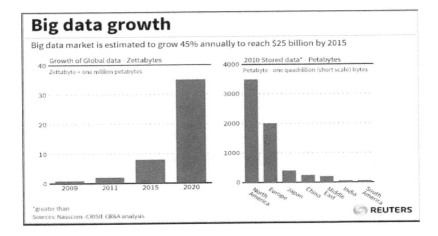

With all of this data, how in the world do we stop information overload?

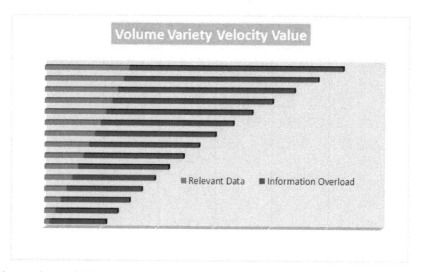

Discussion of big data; what is and what is not big data

One of the first examples of big data was the census taken by the Romans during the time of Christ. Another is the U.S. census that took hold in 1790. Big data is a census in those vast sources of information combined into a database or data processing engine. Those billions of pieces of information are sorted and processed to allow for specific search results.

Many people comment on "Big Data" but the true meaning is inadequately comprehended. Big data is often just large sets of data. For the moment, let us review the records for real property for the Harris County Appraisal District. HCAD has real property records for over 1.6 million properties, with perhaps 100 fields of data for each property. This is about 160 million bits of data, so it must be Big Data, right? The answer is no, this would not be considered Big Data because of the size of the country and the limited number of fields of data. Perhaps a list of all the apartments in the United States would be considered Big Data. Again, the answer is no. There are not enough fields and diversity of data in a list of apartment properties.

Examples of Big Data

Factors which impact whether data is big data include the size of the data set, number and variety of users contributing to the data set, and the number and variety of fields of data. Whether the data is structured can also contribute to it being considered Big Data. Let us consider a source of big data that is derived from one company, but overlaid with data from multiple contributors.

All Google searches, the page selected after the search, the location of the person searching, and possibly the identity of the person is an example of what makes big data. If 500 million people each performed three Google searches a day for 15 years, there will have been 8.2 trillion Google searches. For each search, Google knows the location of the person searching, the phrase used for the search and the page(s) selected. Google also knows who did many of the searches.

Predicting a flu outbreak faster than doctors or the Center for Disease Control (CDC) is one way data has been used. Google was able to predict a flu epidemic well before the CDC. The Google search data can be used to study recent events and causation, and to make educated predictions. Google could use information on searches prior to an election and find an indication of the winner. For example, do you think many Donald Trump voters searched for Hillary Clinton the day before the election?

Let's consider an example closer to the housing industry.

Housing and Big Data

During 2007 and 2008 there was an incredible level of optimism regarding the ever-increasing value of single-family homes. While it is often darkest before the dawn, optimism typically peaks with prices. Except during the Katrina event, apartment absorption in Houston, Texas dropped to almost zero, during a housing boom. Google searches related to housing would have changed enormously over the period from 2007 to 2016. A possible list of searches over this period would have included: 1) flipping houses, 2) refinance and pull out cash, 3) buy houses with no money down, 4) attorney to stop foreclosure, 5) bankruptcy, 6) apartments for rent, and 7) apartments for rent – no credit check required. Do you think it is possible that Google could have called the housing bust earlier than the government, simply based on search phrases? It is probable that Google search phrases are a leading indicator of economic activity.

Personal Big Data

Retailers are using information on purchases to customize coupons and offers given customers. A father was furious when Target sent his teenage daughter coupons and offers appropriate for a pregnant woman. The father was outraged that Target was promoting products to children which were normally sold to women. His daughter had not yet finished high school. Dad cooled off, at least with Target, when he found out his daughter had purchased a pregnancy test there.

Big data includes all purchases using credit or debit cards and frequent buyer cards. This data is sold to aggregators. If you want a list of who is buying guns, fishing rods, diapers, or Campbell soup, it is available. You can also find out the age, marital status, home value, number of children, and psychographic profile for each of the prospects. Perhaps you are trying to sell expensive fly-fishing vacations in Alaska. Getting a list of everyone who has purchased any fishing gear in the last year would be a good start. However, it would include a large number of people who could not afford the vacation you are selling. A review of psychographic data on prior clients and the home value of fishing gear buyers would allow you to target your list to those most likely to purchase your fishing vacation.

Will Big Data Go Too Far

Many of the vast data bases are separated into various tables that do not connect. They include toll road charges, credit card charges, purchases tracked by stores, cell phone calls (including the person you called and your location at the time of the call), medical records, tax returns, travel records, real estate transactions, marital status, number of children, vehicles owned, past residences and your estimated psychographic profile. Now, let's assume it was possible to combine the phone records of all calls since 2001, all purchases made by each person for the same period (other than cash or check), their housing history, travel history, and the profile of people they called or received calls from. To our knowledge, this database does not exist. However, the components are available if required by court order. This data could be used innocently to target people who do not live near an apartment complex but frequently stay overnight near the property and often have dinner at a restaurant near the property. It could also be used to target people who work near the property but do not live near the property. After the first list was compiled (work near but do not live near), it could be filtered to identify those who have income appropriate for the property based on shopping history or psychographic profile.

A scary use of this data would be to track anyone who visits a membership organization and track their phone calls, domicile, shopping patterns and purchases, history of communications with persons of interest, domestic and foreign travel, their daily routine based on their cell phone location, and toll road payments.

Big data is not immediately accessible to the public. However, much of the data discussed (excluding the Google search data) is available for purchase. Apartment owners and investors can use finely honed mailing lists to target prospective tenants. The first step would be to assemble a psychographic profile for the existing residents. Each household is coded as one of 88 categories by a Nielsen subsidiary Claritas. The categories include "blue bloods" (old money) and "shot guns and pickups." After categorizing your existing residents, you could develop marketing material and a marketing plan to target this niche. It could also include minor changes to the property and amenities to better serve the target residents. Marketing could include direct mail to the target categories within an appropriate distance of your property.

Another example would be to get data regarding the purchases made by their residents. Combing this information could provide insights for an amenity or make changes that would be popular with the residents. For example, if 40% of the residents spend money on golf a putting green may be worthwhile. If a number of the residents spend money on high-end cooking utensils and accessories, it might be worthwhile to offer an upgraded appliance package with a longer lease at a higher rental rate.

Conclusion

Big Data is here to stay. When people become aware of the volume of publicly available information, it often upsets them. However, this is the reality of living in the modern world (your alternative is to live off the grid, engage only in cash transactions, be unemployed, etc.) There are many positive and effective ways to use data. There are also strong limitations on private companies that could use the information inappropriately. The magnitude of data available and the uncertainty about what information is available are the first challenges in acquiring and analyzing big data. Some of the data is relatively unstructured, which makes it quite difficult to analyze. Organizing and analyzing unstructured data is an area of intense research and activity. Even if data is in well-organized tables, the volume of data and number of fields compound the difficulty in extracting meaningful information.

So if you are a large institutional company, get ready to embrace big data. Hire a Chief Technology or Data Officer if you are ready to go big, or a well-skilled data hound with some technology background if you are ready to dip your toe in the water. For medium sized companies, look to third party vendors who can provide data storage and unique technological processing applications to make you more efficient. These tools can separate you from the competition. For the smaller companies and work from home entrepreneurs, look to pre-load applications already pre-filled with data, client leads and processing applications to provide you the tools the big companies have, but do not share.

We hope you find the book a little entertaining, a little informative and more importantly give you some tools to be better at what you do. Shaving a few seconds, a few minutes and a few hours on individual processes in your workday can be just what you need to be more successful, make more money!

BIG DATA IN REAL ESTATE
BE A MILLIONAIRE

1

LEGACY OR NEWLY-FOUND INVESTMENT OPPORTUNITY

Why has real estate ownership been so important to the human race? Why does someone own a 20,000 square foot house when he cannot actually use all of the space? Why do the wealthy spend so much money to own multi-million dollar homes? Why does real estate investment make more millionaires than any other industry? How do real estate millionaires and billionaires, who transfer the wealth to their heirs, provide an incentive to help their heir increase their family's wealth further?

Since Adam and Eve entered the pristine Garden of Eden, real estate has been all about location, location, location. Once the partnership was driven out of heaven on earth, Adam and Eve could never return. For thousands of generations, the patriarch, i.e., the family member who created the wealth from real estate, passed ownership to their heirs. You certainly cannot take it with you when you die.

For centuries, in many cultures the oldest male son inherited the bulk of the family's estate. The rest of the family members were at the mercy of the generosity of the eldest. Many times, the younger siblings moved away from the family estates. A review of history found that America provided an opportunity for European non-legacy siblings in the 1800s to establish real estate ownership and a legacy of wealth built on that foundation. Consequently, many of them prospered.

Monks built monasteries and vineyards that now produce the world's leading wines. Manhattan became the trading hub of the world and rental rates appreciated to some of the highest in the world. Massive farms in the Midwest were established and production quickly outpaced national demand, allowing farmers to send agricultural products throughout the world.

Germany's Fugger Foundation has maintained wealth beyond imagination for over five centuries. Countess Maria Elisabeth Thun-Fugger, the foundation's chair, reported that converting cash and assets to real estate provided illiquid assets that subsequent generations could not squander. That wealth has weathered world wars, investment fads and economic crisis.

The next two decades will see the greatest transfer of generational wealth the world has ever seen. Baby boomers were born post World War II, between the years of 1946 and 1964. That aging United States population, upon their death, will transfer massive wealth to their heirs through real estate.

If you have been in real estate for some time, you probably have heard Mark Twain's opinion, "Buy land, they're not making it anymore." Real estate is a tangible asset. You can touch it, see it, build on it, enhance it and manage it. Renters provide a return "on" and "of" the investment. Return on investment is a profitability measure, calculated by taking the profit and dividing it by the cost or value of the asset. This investment benchmark can then be compared against other investments, like paper assets or precious metals. The return of the investment is the rate at which the cost or value of the asset is returned to the owner. The combination of return on and of the investment provides the basis for determining investment-real-estate-purchase decisions.

Appreciation is the rate at which an asset increases in value. Every real estate investor is betting that the price they purchased the asset for will increase. Most real estate investors make their fortunes on the "buy side" of the equation. Investors acquiring assets below-market levels outperform those paying retail (current market price). The acquisition at below-market pricing provides for instant equity and has enhanced the balance sheet of thousands of savvy investors.

Precious metals, cattle, and oil have created millionaire investors, but not at the scale of real estate investors. Transparency in those markets provides a unilateral foundation of information from which to make purchase and investment decisions. Commodities are not only being traded by the largest investment firms in the world, but also by housewives and college students in Des Moines, Iowa. Rarely do investors actually take possession of gold and silver, but rather they accept a paper certificate of ownership for the precious metals that sit in a vault in Australia.

Paper assets like stocks and bonds go up and down, not only due to a company's economic performance, but also due to social and economic factors outside of a company's control. For many investors, daily trading of paper assets has become a way of life and the fortunes made can dissipate in days if the betting strategy goes awry in times of social and economic upheavals. Further, in paper asset trading, the legacy of investment prowess through generations has not been well proven; hence, the reasons why many hedge fund managers invest substantial amounts of wealth into their homes and tangible assets to leave to their heirs.

So how do investors make wealth on the buy side of the equation? There are more Facebook users than there are real estate assets in the United States. But the value of U.S. real estate exceeds the value of the U.S. Treasury. Buildings in highly desirable locations can sell for over $2,000 per square foot, while the same building at another location can sell for $200 per square foot. Two homes can sit across from each other on the same street. One has a Scottsdale address and the other a Phoenix address. The Scottsdale, Arizona, address mandates a 10%+ premium. At an intersection, the "going to work" side of the street caters to tenants desiring breakfast services, while the "going home" side of the street caters to retail tenants desiring dinner services. So how do both savvy investors process the infinite number of influences and data points that affect real estate pricing to build legacy investments that last generations?

If you have been fortunate enough to have a legacy investment, there is a good chance that your wealth was not built from processing Big Data. Very likely, it was the result of decades of working long hours, personal sacrifice and the need to be the best. Now your goal can be to sustain that wealth and build on it. Social media, mass marketing and target marketing can be manipulated through sophisticated tools to advertise your product or service unlike anything that was available 10 years ago. Think of the home phone. With less than 40% of U.S. homes having a home phone, companies need to be proactive in changing the way they do business.

What would your target audience think if you reached them via cell phone, LinkedIn, Facebook, Instagram and a flyer that showed up in their office all over a two-week period? We talked with a sophisticated commercial mortgage banker who reported he completed a refinancing with only one phone call to the owner and all other interactions were through text messages.

The days of marketing to a single client via multiple lunches, meetings, and golf outings is changing. Professionals reach more people, process more transactions and exponentially increase their revenue while working fewer hours than their father and mother did.

What would you do with more money and more free time? Many successful real estate investors think working more hours gives them the upper edge. Obviously owning 30 investment properties takes considerably more time than owning one. Knowing market statistics (listings, days on market, pendings, price trends, etc.) makes you a smarter investor. Being a part-time real estate investor, looking for newfound fortunes, takes away from family and social time. But associating with people with positive attitudes helps breed success, and the long term benefits from real estate investments can be your newfound legacy to your future generations.

If you are looking to reposition a commercial asset, follow the lead of innovators like Andrew Segal of Boxer Properties. Under his leadership, the company has repositioned numerous real estate assets by creating shortened lease agreements and the ability for on-site management to quickly execute a lease, finishing out small office suites for quick tenant occupancy, providing a competitive insurance brokerage atmosphere to get the best rates, and tracking utility rates to take advantage of off-peak rates. Real time management, coupled with some of the lowest operating costs in the industry, has made Boxer an industry leader.

While buildings may depreciate and need to be renovated or even razed, land is something that cannot be replaced. The best advice is know your real estate market. That could be a subdivision, zip code, or local area. When looking at larger geographical areas, focus on special land use types, e.g., medical buildings, triple-net leases (triple net NNN properties are typically single tenant buildings where the tenant pays all expenses, including building repairs), leased assets, car washes, etc. Knowing not only the geographic area, but also the unique property types, provides additional expertise to make a new investment a win from the time of purchase. We cannot stress enough that money is made on the buy side, i.e., the purchase price is below other properties of equal utility.

Below-market purchase prices can carry an investor through economic downturns and increases in vacancy. These acquisitions also create a future "piggy bank" for investors, using that excess equity through home equity loans, refinancing, and collateral for lines of credit to expand an investor's real estate empire.

So what is the downside as real estate market trends tend to change in slow cycles? While stocks can change 5% in one week with fifty-two-week highs and lows over 100% variable, rarely do real estate trends change double digit in one year. Government and banking regulations can overly inflate or deflate a real estate market. Typically that occurs across all property types and locations. Knowledge of federal banking policies and rates is as important as knowing that a new listing was advertised today in your target market. Ten and thirty-year bond, LIBOR and mortgage rate trends should be reviewed periodically, as they have a direct effect on real estate investing. These can be viewed on numerous websites: bankrate.com, data.worldbank.org, global-rates.com. Find your favorite website and visit regularly.

So, let's assume you have already purchased a real estate investment and you want to be the next Trump. The local market is in a stability stage, i.e., no measurable changes in values. Few listings on the market and foreclosures are non-existent. Vacancies are staying around 8.0%. There could be other options:

1. Is there land to build new product? The opportunity to build a real estate product where cost plus land pricing is below finished product provides that up front equity you are looking for.

2. Are there borrowers that need financing help? Second mortgages provide yields higher than first mortgages and can provide the returns you are looking for.

3. Are there renovation opportunities? Not all tenants and owners maintain properties equally. Looking for dilapidated real estate and bringing those assets to market condition can provide that needed equity, again, that you are looking for.

4. Expand your coverage. Real estate cycles in this global economy tend to have excess downsides when markets decline. Look at Detroit, which in 2016 was reported to have a population similar to the community's level in 1950. The Census Bureau reported that the last time Detroit wasn't in the Top 20 was 1850. While the 2015 population decline was half of a percent, real estate pricing declined around 10% for the

same period. There are "contrarian" investors making significant investments in Detroit real estate, focusing on purchasing assets sufficiently "below market," to offset further declines.

5. Look for assets that can produce pricing premiums. Do one-story homes sell for more than two-story homes? Do four-bedroom homes sell for a premium versus three-bedroom homes of the same size? Upgrades in bathrooms and kitchens can provide returns in excess of cost.

This research can allow investors to purchase real estate at below market rates and build immediate equity. Much of this information can be found at www.enricheddata.com.

What about apartments and the new trend of co-habitation? Connected homes are typically categorized as duplex, tri-plex, townhouse, condominium, and apartments. Building permits typically categorize them as single family, 2 units, 3 to 4 units and 5+ units. Purchasing a multi-unit complex can provide numerous benefits, including the ability to rent out the other units and stay in a unit for a reduced rent, or even free. Renting out a bedroom is a trend that became effective with the ability to market through on-line services like Airbnb. Even college students are renting out their rooms during the summer when they go home to visit mom and dad.

Real estate, like other assets, can appreciate over time. The "time is money" phrase bodes well for young real estate investors. Starting young investing in real estate allows time for appreciation. And the cyclical nature of financial investments tends to be less of a consideration over decades of ownership.

So now you are ready to sell your investment. How should it be positioned to command the highest price? Is it equally important to sell it fast? Should you employ a professional real estate agent? Any renovations needed?

A few tried and true factors may be in your favor.

- A sale to an owner occupant typically commands a higher price than a sale to an investor. Owner occupants may even pay premiums if there are building attributes and functionalities that appeal to their social, business, and spatial needs.

- Remaining lease term is a major factor in determining pricing. A 10-year remaining lease term demands a price premium over a 9-year term. A 5-year remaining lease term demands a price premium over a 4-year term. But little pricing changes occur for a 10-year versus an 11-year term or a 5-year versus a 6-year term. That is because commercial lending terms typically have 20 to 25-year amortization terms, but the loan balance is due in the 5th or 10th year. A lease structure mimicking or exceeding the 5 to 10-year "call" provides additional lender security. An investor may want to restructure the lease term with the tenant prior to a sale.

- When prospective buyers tour properties, favorable site and smell attributes can enhance demand. Dead or dying landscape, musty odors, and stains on paint and carpets can easily deter buyers. Cosmetic upgrades are typically low cost repairs and curing deferred maintenance (postponed repair items that are needed) can help if investors look to sell properties at price premiums. And nothing beats the smell of fresh baked cookies.

- Keep it clean. Unwanted clutter is a potential sign of mismanagement.

- Maximize marketing efforts. Relying only on the local multiple listing service (MLS) may not showcase your property to all prospective buyers. Online advertising through Trulia, Craigslist, and other websites is important to maximize exposure to buyers. Building a website just to market your asset could be as low as $10. Email flyers to your friends and have them resend the flyer out to their friends can get you needed exposure.

- And get ready to be a manager!

It is now time to discuss real estate as generational wealth and who people, of any age, can influence and even start, real estate trends.

It is difficult to have assets like stocks and bonds carry through legacies. But real estate, that is another story. Consider the local wine merchant in Europe that inherited the family's vineyard and winery for the 20 plus generation (https://grapecollective.com/articles/count-sebastiano-capponi-villa-calcinaia). Tried and true methods of agriculture have now brought the unique tastes to the world through internet orders and fast on-time delivery. The family's economic stability is as strong as it was in the 1400's. And the family's daughters are now taking the asset into the next decade.

Women now have significant opportunity in real estate careers, from residential home sales, to mortgage origination, to property managers, who oversee engineers, porters and maintenance professionals. Starting out as a receptionist and secretary and moving to a Senior Property Manager overseeing over 500,000 square feet of high-rise office and mixed use commercial is obtainable for those women willing to make the commitment. A sales agent can grow into the owner of one of the largest upscale residential brokerage firms in the country. Commercial Real Estate Women (CREW) is an excellent group with which to expand your network. And if you have a special talent for giving presentations, speakers are sought after across the country to speak at monthly local events.

Let's talk about upcoming women in the real estate industry. Ivanka Trump is Executive Vice President (EVP) of the Trump Organization. Will her direction move that company's $10B market capitalization to $20B? Then there is a professional like Marilyn Jordan Taylor, the dean of the University Of Pennsylvania School Of Design. She was the first woman to head the leadership of the Urban Land Institute (ULI), from 2005 to 2007. Barbara Corcoran is a self-made multi-millionaire real estate investor and went on to be a celebrity on Shark Tank. Mary Ann Tighe is CEO of CBRE, the largest commercial brokerage firm in the world, Tristate Area. Her management is taking that global organization to the next level by integrating Big Data with Technology and providing tools in simple, easy-to-use applications to increase her staff's productivity. Debra Cafaro is chairman and CEO of Ventas, a $20 billion health care Real Estate Investment Trust (REIT). Wellington Denahan leads another REIT, Annaly Capital. And of course there is Jennifer Miller, the wife of one of the authors, who grew from a receptionist position to managing multi-million dollar mixed use properties, high-rise commercial real estate, and managing rental property. And our good friend Zee, who adopted her grandchildren to raise them and then after reaching 50+ years of age obtained her real estate license and now sell homes as an agent to help enhance her family's economic security.

Although there is lots of room for growth, opportunities in the real estate profession are prime for women. Owning and managing residential real estate is the simplest form of business. Marketing enhancements in recent years allow potential renters from the world over to view local lease opportunities, e.g., Trulia.com. Rental homes with six-months or longer lease periods are the typical investor's preference and websites like VRBO.com and AirBnB.com have transformed vacation rentals. From remote Colorado mountain retreats, to two-bedroom flats in New York, fully-furnished rental opportunities can be found within minutes. And booking is as easy as any hotel reservation. Property managers post photos, property characteristics, nearby attractions and local activities, while managing occupants who typically lease for 3 to 7 day rentals. Property owners can benefit not only from the revenue but also occasional use of the home for themselves. In high density and expensive cities like New York and San Francisco, home rentals with larger space can be rented for less than mid to high-range hotels.

Learn by associating with real estate leaders by joining clubs and attending professional association seminars, attending classes put on by business schools and reading real estate blogs and internet publications. Building Owners and Managers Association (BOMA), Appraisal Institute (AI), Institute Real Estate Management (IREM), and others are organizations that showcase talent.

There are numerous seminars put on by successful real estate entrepreneurs, like Rich Dad (www.richdad.com). These are not only informational, but a way to crowdsource opportunities and relationship.

When we segment the U.S. population by age, the categories have unique buying and renting habits. The following discussion should provide some overview of how these age groups influence real estate. Knowing which age groups are heavily weighted in a market is important to influencing investment underwriting criteria.

Baby Boomers

This group, born between the years of 1946 and 1964, purchased big homes for their families, but are now downsizing as they enter their empty nester phase as the kids move out. In the first decade of the twenty-first century, the average home sizes increased because of their desire for bigger homes. But when will they retire is a big question, as many people are working well into traditional retirement years. If boomers downsize as they enter empty nest and retirement periods, there could be an adverse effect on the premium housing market. This group did not save for retirement and their underfunded pensions, if available to any in this group, will likely fall below payout expectations due to the fact that government and businesses have incorrectly projected rates of returns and funding amounts. For most baby boomers their home is their biggest asset. And most will tap the equity in that asset to fund retirement, and there are not enough buyers in the next generation to soak up that inventory.

And boomers reflect a number of single head-of-household homeowners, over 25% of the housing stock. That limits the amount of home they can buy. And urbanization requires a higher priced home per square foot, supporting smaller homes. Boomers will need to be creative to create home equity and should consider co-habitation, co-investing and other shared ownership options.

Boomers will look to jettison their burgeoning expenses by paying off their mortgage, lowering utility and property tax expenses, renovate their home rather than lose the funds associated with selling and buying a smaller home (there are significant 'lost' costs when selling and buying a home), or downsize. If they decide to move, it will likely be close to family and friends and in areas that provide walkability.

Generation X

Born from 1965 to 1980, this group tends to be entrepreneurial and individualistic. They tend to be more concerned about their local community's issues. They are less committed to big business and government than to those around them. They had a huge swing in home ownership rates; in 2004, they had the highest ownership rates in history, but it fell to the lowest in 2015. The boom-bust era fostered distrust in economic policies of both government and business. Because so many opted out, either voluntarily or were forced out, they did not have the opportunity to buy "move-up" housing, which is a typically larger and more expensive home. The group is smaller than millennials, about 83 million versus 87 million, and has an additional financial burden: their children are living in their homes longer. The additional utility, food, and other charges bear on Generation X's ability to save. And many in this group don't see renting as a waste of money.

The 2007/2008 recession pushed many in this group outside of the home ownership market. About 4.2 million homeowners, almost a quarter of this generation, lost their homes in the housing crisis. And that left a void for investment real estate buyers. As a result, REIT and investment companies had expanded during their prime investment years.

This is the first generation to use computers for just about everything. They will look at least nine websites to review house purchase opportunities. They would rather have a home office than an extra bedroom. But they prefer calling for fast-food delivery, rather than ordering on-line. They will tend to shop longer than other generations, being skeptical of great deals and pushy sales professionals.

This group's retirement ideas are not focused on a rocking chair on the front porch. They want to be engaged; proximity to restaurants and walking areas are important to this group. While this group typically opts for hotels versus Airbnb or VRBO, they are mobile and big motor homes are attractive to them.

Millennials Act Like No Generation Before

The generation prior to millennials sought home ownership as a right of passage. However, millennials do not view homeownership the same way. Co-habitation brings a communal lifestyle where twenty somethings can play video games, watch movies, and eat together. Born from 1980 to 2000, this generation is the largest potential homeownership group ever. However, sought-after lifestyles found in cities like New York, Paris and San Francisco have home prices well out of reach for this young group so they co-habitat in smaller home footprints than ever before. Large 3 story historical brownstones, once the domicile of wealthy urbanites, are now renovated into 9 unit flats (one-level apartments or condominiums) that house two and three residents and likely, even a couple of dogs per unit. These residents live as much outside their homes, as inside.

And their lifestyles are affecting the financial technology (Fintech) industry like never before. They do not want to use checks and are expecting significant changes in the banking industry. They believe that innovation to banking will not come from within, but from outside. Millennials are looking towards fintech (financial technology) start-ups to disrupt the banking industry. Levering technology to millennials is key for future growth. Mobile applications and social media drive the $10 billion in changes to the banking industry since 2010.

The preferred selection for most millennials is areas where smart cars, walking, biking and skateboarding can connect them from their home to bars, movie theaters, restaurants, open space parks and trail systems. They prefer quality over quantity. The best example of how millennials think follows:

> The human resource (HR) director at a large beverage distribution company in one of the largest cities in the U.S. was approached by his 26-year old top-of-the-line truck driver. The driver informed the HR director that he was putting in his notice to quit. The HR director was astounded, as he told the driver that he was one of the company's leading employees, showered with raises and accolades for top performance. And that his $50,000+ salary would continue to grow and could lead to management position. He then asked the driver, "What are you going to do?" The driver informed him that he had been living with his parents and saved enough money to take off three months and hike the Appalachian Trail!" After that, he would re-evaluate his employment opportunities.

Obviously, with focus on life choices, millennials will choose home ownership much later in life. College debt, incomes that does not escalate as fast as prior generations, and low credit scores, many times due to poor credit history, does not allow this generation to purchase homes early in life. This could result in lower home ownership rates nationally for decades. But the population in the 50 largest U.S. cities will continue to attract this generation and with them comes their toys, i.e., technology and applications.

Therefore, catering rental housing to this significant group is a great investment strategy. Homes with wifi, the ability to showcase large televisions, and numerous power outlets are just some of the options millennials desire. Choice of location can spin-off from their college choices, as this group has more college degrees than any prior generation. As they spend more time at school, they tend to build a core relationship around their classmates and dating partners. This group will also have fewer children. These factors point to smaller home footprints in urban markets with active social and retail facilities nearby. Older urban areas are prime renovation opportunities that are attractive to millennials. Conversion of one-story rambler homes into duplexes with small patios is an excellent investment.

In June 2015, the Census Bureau reported millennials exceeded the number of baby boomers. And as they stay in school longer, wait later in life to get married and to have children, they will also have to rent, as obtaining a mortgage for high priced urban housing is elusive. But this diverse generation, when they co-habitat, has significant disposable incomes to purchase the most recent technologies and applications. And while they strive to work no more than 40 hours per week, they use these technology applications for instant gratification. Hit songs, videos, photos and games go viral in hours. They spend hundreds of dollars on earphones to get the best quality experience. Visual and hearing experiences are top off-work selections. And rental homes that are located close to entertainment venues are preferred.

This is reviving urban centers. Boutique clothing stores, convenience stores stocked with fresh fruit and yogurt rather than candy and Icees, and non-chain restaurants where patrons order and pick their food from the counter and eat in open patio areas, are becoming common place. But this cash-less society who use debit cards to pay for Uber rides to and from the bars and nightlife tend to live a healthier lifestyle, can expect to live well over 80 years.

In order for smaller cities to prevent the "brain drain," i.e. young educated people moving to larger cities, they will need to provide live, work, and play urban centers. New home product in townhouse, duplex, triplex and 4+ unit structures near revitalized center cores will attract this new generation. Nightlife is a key attraction to keeping them engaged. Boutique hotels, fitness and wellness facilities in a downtown setting are also needed for those towns to thrive.

With over 20 million households spending at least 30% of their income on rent and utilities, the home ownership rate may quickly surpass the 50-year low. Millennials are saddled with record college debt and a flat job market for a decade. The rising affordability issue will result in more density and the need for expansion in the Low Income Housing Credit program. This requires local and federal governments to assist investors in providing these housing alternatives.

Income growth will determine whether millennials become homeowners at the rates of prior generations. Stagnant income, which was evident in the first half of the 2010 decade, will not allow this generation to purchase the typical home in urban cities. They will have to opt for smaller, affordable housing. However, this product does not have to come with meaningless upgrades. Eye catching built-in wine refrigerators, Ninja blending bars, flush-mounted TVs, mini-organic gardens growing wheat grass, and porcelain tile that looks like wood or glass can revitalize a space. Tiny homes don't have to be boring spaces!

For those 62-year-old real estate professionals, having a millennial on the team can make all the difference in a producer's or even a company's longevity. These millennials live and breathe technology while looking for instant "self-gratification" in work, play, and social circles.

Generation Z

Born after 2001, Generation Z is the most culturally diverse American generation. They grew up with HD TVs, video games, and cell phones. Their connectivity to their friends and people around the world is through their hand held devices. They are as apt to text someone at their same restaurant table than talk to them. They have changed the economics of toy making, as virtual reality interactive games have captured their focus. As they enter the world of real estate ownership and rental, they know what they want and where they want it. And that may not be where their family is located, because they know how to connect to their loved ones in ways never before available. They can connect multiple times in a day.

National findings released in 2014 by Better Homes and Gardens® Real Estate revealed "this generation of teens ages 13-17, part of Generation Z, is very traditional in their views toward homeownership and is willing to give up modern luxuries for the mainstream definition of "the American dream."

Gen Z teens indicate that homeownership is the most important factor in achieving the American dream. The second factor is the desire to graduate from college, followed by getting married and having children.

They have never known how to roll down a car window with a knob, how to make a phone call from a pay phone on the street corner, or how to play Pac Man on a big machine. How about processing a picture at the corner camera store? They have it all at their fingertips and they know how to use processed big data efficiently and effectively. They know which retailers have the best sales instantly. They are constantly notified of what is happening around them through updates from websites. They need cloud storage like no generation before and a lot of it.

More than half of this group will graduate from college and own a pet. They tend to be entrepreneurial and they know the need to save money. As investors look to the future, Generation Z will decide how real estate is affected by their lifestyle, work, and play choices. Developers and remodelers will need to look at technology applications integrated into those homes and work environments. The physical and digital worlds are the same to this group; they expect to make changes in a positive way. Their saving habits, along with wealth transfers from prior generations, should make them the wealthiest Americans of any generation. But unlike prior generations, that does not translate into larger homes. Thoughtful analysis of this group's habits needs to be monitored in real time in order to provide real estate choices that are attractive to them.

Investment Conclusion

As an investor looking to residential real estate to make you financially independent, you need to know the socio-economic characteristics of the rental and sales market where that property is located. These age groups look at real estate occupancy differently, and the aging of these groups will change the influences on both new and resale real estate. These factors also affect retail buying trends, average size office characteristics, and how manufacturers deliver goods to not only retailers, but directly to consumers. Knowing who is in your market and what influences they have in real estate trends is important to making money in real estate.

BIGGEST INVESTMENT THE TYPICAL FAMILY MAKES IN A LIFETIME

Let us review why you want to buy a home and possibly investment real estate. Whether it is a 3% or 20% down payment, the purchase of a home is typically the largest investment most families make in their lifetime. Dave Ramsey suggests you could save up money to pay cash. But, if you don't have cash, take out no more than a 15-year loan with a payment no more than 25% of your take-home income. Many borrowers do end up in a debtor's spiral with little possibility of cashing out. Thirty-year mortgages, draining equity through home equity loans and refinancing every few years to use the money on disposable assets is no way to build wealth. Many think a "debtor's prison" is the inability to borrow money due to bad credit.

The latest financial crisis should be no surprise to the bankers who helped cause it. No doubt, we will see future financial crises, as liberal debt policies lead to lax lending, lax lending leads to increased foreclosures and increased foreclosures lead to bank failures.

For centuries, money changers and lenders have been a necessary evil to help increase personal, family, community and even the country's wealth. Without bankers, life as we know it would not exist. Ancient Greeks developed mathematical models to calculate compound interest. In the 13th century, Western Europe began developing numerals to document loan amounts and interest rates. Contract terms were used to engage the parties and there were repercussions if principle and interest were not repaid.

Philip IV, ironically known as "Philip the Fair," was the king of France in the early 1300's and was so indebted to the Knights Templar that he had them tried for heresy and killed. That must have been a lot of debt! While stringing up lenders is not a course of action to take, numerous government laws have been enacted to help the consumer. Fair lending practices allow transparency, and consumers can review everything from their credit report to the appraisal. Fill out multiple on-line loan applications, and within the hour, phone calls will come with promises of best rates and quick closings. Buyers should fill out at least three applications, and then determine their best options.

So how do spouses manage their finances to purchase rental houses and expand their wealth? How do individuals expand their minimal real estate inheritance to owning a vast real estate portfolio? Most use leverage.

Leverage is a simple concept. In terms of building asset value, using debt at interest rates below the cash flow yield of the asset (positive leverage) causes wealth to accelerate. Large real estate investment trusts (REITs) and investment firms purchase assets at current known rates of return. Then firms borrow money at lower rates than the asset's rate of return, using the yield spread (difference between the debt versus the cash on cash return of the investment) to enhance their investment return.

Who wins if the market continues to perform? The borrower does because he obtains rates of return above other investment alternatives. In times of market appreciation, investors obtain annual cash on cash rates of return above lender's rates and incur appreciation that allows the investor to eventually sell the property well above the original purchase price.

Who loses if the market does not perform? The investor does first and the lender second. The lender typically has the first lien and forecloses as soon as the borrower cannot pay the mortgage. The lender then loses if the asset value cannot be sold at or above the mortgage amount.

So is it better to be the lender or the investor? Since the Knights Templar, a select few thought being on the lender's side was the safest investment until the King of France stepped in and changed the rules. Even today, governments change the rules – but most recently to protect the lenders who are "too big to fail."

Back to the family who just wants to buy a house. In India, lenders leverage the "gold reserves" of the family as well as the real estate assets. In many areas of the world, 50+ year mortgages can be procured, but are typically limited to 30 years in the U.S. So when newlyweds purchase their first home, what should be their goal? Well, there are some simple recommendations that will help them.

1. Pay a little extra each month to the principle! The cost of forgoing a dinner out and applying that each month to extra principle payments can take years off the mortgage term.

2. Maintain the property. If the property is ever resold, new buyers will pay at or above market for well-maintained assets that do not have deferred maintenance. If you are not an expert, data is being processed on internet websites, like Angie's List, that rates vendors and can help you make the best maintenance and renovation decisions.

3. Enhance the property. While remodeling kitchens and baths are bantered about as having the highest returns on investment, other more simple enhancements can provide your family and resale potential excellent returns. Mass data is processed through http://www.remodeling.hw.net/cost-vs-value/2015/ and they suggest steel entry replacement doors provide value returns above cost. This is also a great security feature for a family not interested in selling anytime soon.

4. Protest your property taxes every year! Assessors use big data to determine your house's assessed value. But are they concluding your house could be assessed higher than your neighbor's house? Do local laws call for both market value and "equalization," whereby houses in your neighborhood have to be equally assessed? Websites like www.cutmytaxes.com quickly evaluate big data to determine if your home is over-assessed. Real estate taxes are one of a homeowner's biggest annual expenses, and you need to stay on top of it, because government continues to get bigger and is grabbing for more revenue from homeowners.

5. Stay on top of your utility costs. Deregulation across most of the U.S. has allowed homeowners the opportunity to competitively bid utility services with multiple vendors. Review vendor's utility charges annually. And look for opportunities to make your home more efficient: seal windows, fluctuate air conditioning and heating temperatures when you are not home (preprogrammed electronic thermostats easily return the value above cost in the investment), plant trees to create shade from the sun, prune trees in cold climates, and use fans to supplement cooling.

We are regularly asked by non-real estate professionals, "Should I get my real estate license even though I am not in the real estate industry?" And our answer is always, "Yes, if you just buy a house or help a friend buy a house, it will pay for your time and investment." Much more money could come from you helping multiple friends and then buying yourself a house and then an investment house. That 3% commission applied to the price of the house would go a long way in creating your financial stability.

Everyone has some real estate background knowledge. Owning versus renting a home comes with a significant difference in time commitment. Yard upkeep, structural repairs and replacement of broken or outdated fixtures and appliances is considerable when owning a home. Then add a pool, kids (and do not forget about their friends who visit) and a puppy to add to the chaos. Now you have a real time commitment! On top of that, you are thinking about buying a rental house? Are you crazy!

If you do invest in real estate, you will soon find it is like having another sibling, annoying, but well worth it, although, we have met some investors who view their real estate holdings as a more important relationship than their children. They become obsessed to a level where reality is mirrored by the fact that the real estate is not worth what they are suggesting is the value. As a result, many have lost those investments through foreclosure or lawsuits.

To find a home price point target first, most buyers look at entry-level homes. Then they search all listings, pendings, and sales in the selected market. With technology, that does not have to be your immediate community. Search all properties using multiple websites and you'll get to see homes which have lengthy days on market. Downloading the listings into an excel spreadsheet allows sorting and analysis that most websites do not provide. After a few weeks, new listings will be recognized immediately.

Now it is time to get pre-approved for your loan. It will go much smoother when the seller knows you have the financial backing of a lender, better yet, able to pay cash. Cash buyers typically get moved to the front of the list when making offers. A rich uncle, friend with cash and even in-laws can quickly be replaced post-closing with a bank loan.

Before considering rehab opportunities, make sure you are well-connected to painters, drywall installers, electricians, and plumbers. You will pay at least 15% to 25% more if you employ a general contractor to manage the subcontractors, money needed to save in order to increase your return on and of the investment. And do not over-improve; you want to be in the lower one-third of the price category for the submarket, not at the upper end. Lower quality and condition homes tend to get "dragged" up in a market with higher-priced homes, and higher quality and condition homes tend to get "dragged" down by lower priced homes in a neighborhood.

Pay attention to any permits issued on the home that show any past remodeling, whether the roof was replaced and other key metrics that make the home superior or inferior to the average home in the market. While interior finishes are many times the largest cost component of a home, before considering renovations, a cost-benefit analysis has to be completed. The following is a typical breakdown of the cost components of a single-family home:

Table I. Single Family Price and Cost Breakdowns 2015 National Results		
Average Lot Size:		20,129
Average Finished Area:		2,802
I. Sale Price Breakdown	**Average**	**Share of Price**
A. Finished Lot Cost (including financing cost)	$85,139	18.2%
B. Total Construction Cost	$289,415	61.8%
C. Financing Cost	$6,285	1.3%
D. Overhead and General Expenses	$26,345	5.6%
E. Marketing Cost	$3,739	0.8%
F. Sales Commission	$15,104	3.2%
G. Profit	$42,292	9.0%
Total Sales Price	**$468,318**	**100%**
II. Construction Cost Breakdown	**Average**	**Share of Construction Cost**
I. Site Work (sum of A to E)	**$16,092**	**5.6%**
A. Building Permit Fees	$3,601	1.2%
B. Impact Fee	$1,742	0.6%
C. Water & Sewer Fees Inspections	$4,191	1.4%
D. Architecture, Engineering	$4,583	1.6%
E. Other	$1,975	0.7%
II. Foundations (sum of F to G)	**$33,447**	**11.6%**
F. Excavation, Foundation, Concrete, Retaining walls, and Backfill	$32,576	11.3%
G. Other	$871	0.3%
III. Framing (sum of H to L)	**$52,027**	**18.0%**
H. Framing (including roof)	$44,640	15.4%
I. Trusses (if not included above)	$3,884	1.3%
J. Sheathing (if not included above)	$1,238	0.4%
K. General Metal, Steel	$1,272	0.4%
L. Other	$993	0.3%
IV. Exterior Finishes (sum of M to P)	**$43,447**	**15.0%**
M. Exterior Wall Finish	$20,717	7.2%
N. Roofing	$10,069	3.5%
O. Windows and Doors (including garage door)	$12,127	4.2%
P. Other	$534	0.2%
V. Major Systems Rough-ins (sum of Q to T)	**$37,843**	**13.1%**
Q. Plumbing (except fixtures)	$12,302	4.3%
R. Electrical (except fixtures)	$12,181	4.2%
S. HVAC	$12,623	4.4%
T. Other	$738	0.3%
VI. Interior Finishes (sum of U to AE)	**$85,642**	**29.6%**
U. Insulation	$6,467	2.2%
V. Drywall	$11,744	4.1%
W. Interior Trims, Doors, and Mirrors	$12,409	4.3%
X. Painting	$9,002	3.1%
Y. Lighting	$3,517	1.2%
Z. Cabinets, Countertops	$16,056	5.5%
AA. Appliances	$4,463	1.5%
AB. Flooring	$13,367	4.6%
AC. Plumbing Fixtures	$4,465	1.5%
AD. Fireplace	$2,760	1.0%
AE. Other	$1,393	0.5%
VII. Final Steps (sum of AF to AJ)	**$19,567**	**6.8%**
AF. Landscaping	$6,156	2.1%
AG. Outdoor Structures (deck, patio, porches)	$4,349	1.5%
AH. Driveway	$6,240	2.2%
AI. Clean Up	$2,054	0.7%
AJ. Other	$768	0.3%
VIII. Other	**$1,349**	**0.5%**
Total	**$289,415**	**100%**

Special Studies November 2, 2015
By Heather Taylor
NAHB Economics and Housing Policy Group

A typical single-family investor looks at both interior finishes and final steps categories upgrades to increase the value of a home. Let us look at the categories that should be reviewed:

- Insulation – upgrades are easier now than ever with blown-in, thermos-shields and spray foam insulation. Drywall and wall coverings no longer have to be removed in order to implement upgrades. Lower utility bills are a great repayment.

- Drywall – texture over drywall does a great job of hiding imperfections; however, when drywall replacement occurs, matching the texture is an art. Anyone who has had to remove wallpaper has an affinity to not add new wallpaper. Latex based paints make up a majority of the market demand, as new paints feature mildew resistance, low odor emissions, and ease of maintenance. A little bit of paint can go a long way on baseboards and crown molding, improving rooms with a "pop" will capture renters and home-buyer's attention.

- Lighting – both exterior and interior lighting enhancements can be very inexpensive and provide architectural features that can make your home more attractive than the neighbor's. Adding a chandelier to a room can be eye-catching.

- Cabinets, countertops, and freshly-painted cabinets goes a long way in changing the look of a kitchen. While total cabinet replacement is not something for a novice, replacing cabinet doors can be done on a weekend. Countertop replacement requires some expertise, and when undertaken, functionality and durability, as well as look, should be considered.

- Appliances – the cost and installation of a microwave is the easiest. Matching finishes and colors between the refrigerator, microwave and dishwasher will show renters and buyers you place importance on aesthetics, and imply an increased level of management ability.

- Flooring – any property manager of beachfront condominiums knows "carpet is bad!" Rental properties with tile and wood floors have less maintenance than those with carpet. Porcelain is harder and less scratch resistant than ceramic or wood. The selection of flooring material is one of the most important decisions in a remodel. Let's look at some flooring options:

  o Cork Flooring

    Cork is a renewable and eco-friendly resource by peeling off the bark while saving the tree. The material has a number of good characteristics: insulation, sound-proofing, anti-allergenic, resists well against insects, resistant against abrasion, and can be easily cleaned.

o Laminate Flooring

This is a low-cost option from wood or stone. Laminate will show no signs of fading or stains for a decade, it's not easily affected by moisture, and clean-up is easy.

o Linoleum Flooring

A composition of cork wood dust, limestone, recycled wood flour, and linseed oil, linoleum is an environmentally safe choice, resistant from impacts or dents and is fun to walk barefoot on.

o Stone Flooring

Natural stone can be costly. Limestone, clay, granite, pebble, sandstone, slate, travertine and onyx provide varying looks and maintenance requirements. Rehab with stone floors should only be undertaken for upscale homes or in areas where the flooring needs to withstand high temperatures, near fireplaces, stoves, or furnaces.

o Tile Flooring

Porcelain is more durable and requires less maintenance than ceramic, quarry, and mosaic. One of the most important renovation requirements is to seal the grout, as discoloring will otherwise occur. Glazed tiles provide stain-resistance and can also be used around fireplaces, furnaces, and stoves.

o Vinyl Flooring

With a number of varying colors and patterns, vinyl-flooring materials continue to be enhanced. Durable and low cost, this is a good option if your renovation has to keep to a low-cost budget.

o Wood Flooring

Elegant and visually pleasing, sweeping and periodic polishing wood floors will showcase a room. However, water and scratches (even running dogs) can quickly wear down finishes.

- Plumbing Fixtures – new faucets and toilet seats are fairly inexpensive and go a long way to impress renters and buyers.

- Fireplace – This is a tough maintenance item and could require the buyer to bring out a specialized inspector to review. However, most fireplaces provide an excellent frame for floral, candles or other decorative features. Consider adding propane or natural gas with decorative logs to minimize maintenance.

- Landscaping – The first impression that renters and buyers have is from the street. Dead grass and shrubs is a sign of mismanagement. Xeriscaping is landscaping that reduces or eliminates the need for irrigation and should be implemented in all areas. Tree and bushes on the western side of a building can reduce utility bills.

- Patios, Decks, Porches – Many new home builders do not add patios, decks, or porches. However, outdoor living space enhances the social aspects of a home and front porches can enliven a neighborhood as well as encourage homeowners to interact with their neighbors. Stamped concrete is a great aesthetic enhancement to the look and feel, while pavers or tile certainly bring up the quality of the entire home.

- Driveway – Although most homes have wood dividers separating the concrete, wood tends to have a limited economic life. Self-leveling materials are available in varying colors and providing for a superior look and longer economic life. Pressure washing is a low cost and excellent method to enhance the look of older driveways.

- Cleanup – Trash, discolored paint, stains and other items of deferred maintenance can distress renters and buyers. Keep it clean!

Before undertaking any of these upgrades, look at the upper-end home sales in a market to attempt to isolate which upgrades bring a cost-value enhancement. Besides condition, there are other quality variances in homes and by knowing which extra features create value, you can push the rental amount and home price. There is nothing wrong with calling a local residential appraiser and asking them which upgrades can bring the value-add above the cost.

While new home purchases for investment rentals may favor low near term repairs to manage, in appreciating markets resale homes can be more attractive. Rising home prices typically come with rising construction costs. New home builders tend to then provide more expensive homes to the market. This tends to decrease absorption, as a lower percentage of home buyers can then afford those homes. Those purchasing more expensive homes tend to be move-up buyers; they sell their existing home using the equity as their down payment on their new, more expensive home. Those resales provide rental investment opportunities.

Effective property managers employ aggressive marketing strategies to find renters. Online, newspaper, local green sheets and even yard signs should all be employed. Then, screening as to employment and references is important. A long-term tenant is important to an investor's peace of mind. Multiple roommates can bring increased management and maintenance.

Do not want the hassle of being a property manager? Look to invest in a real estate investment trusts (REIT). There are typically two types of REITs: equity (companies own the real estate) and mortgage (company lends on real estate). The National Association of Real Estate Investment Trusts® (NAREIT) is the voice for REITs and real estate companies that are publicly traded. With almost $2 trillion invested by REITs in real estate, the ability to purchase stocks in these companies allows small and large investors to purchase an interest in real estate. Most carry hefty dividends, and more recently, attractive stock pricing has some companies' asset value below the aggregate value of the real estate they own (the company is worth less than the real estate equity). They have also historically tracked or exceeded the S&P performance.

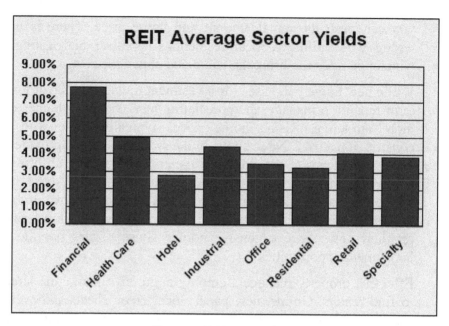

Source: REIT Monitor

Research an industry, real estate sector and REITs to determine if the yields coupled with the opportunity to omit the management component of real estate ownership is attractive.

So keep a level head. Your real estate is only worth what someone will pay for it. And when you die, you cannot take it with you!

REAL ESTATE CYCLES – WHY THEY OCCUR

Everyone has heard of the phrase, "real estate cycles." But understanding why they occur, what influences value change and what variables are important to watch may help investors with the ability to gauge the anticipated future performance of their market and their investment.

The segregation of industry specialists in the real estate industry fragments the data:

- **Property Tax Consultation and Representation:** Millions of property tax protests, by both homeowners and industry specialists occur every year. However, most industry specialists cannot process more than a few thousand clients' protests each year, due to the inability to create a database and client processing system. Big data and client representation processed through computer systems can give property tax consulting firms the necessary tools to represent hundreds of thousands of homeowners. But only a handful of companies have these resources. I know a homeowner with a $14,000,000 assessed value on his house, and he feels compelled to spend 3 days each year preparing for and protesting his real estate taxes. Is this oil and gas executive really prepared to effectively reduce his $62,000 annual tax bill? Homeowners need to understand the laws and provide the necessary documentation to effectively protest their home taxes.

- **Appraisals:** Complex appraisals throughout the U.S. prepared by highly qualified licensed professionals occur annually. The profession is regulated by the U.S. Government through laws mandating state licensing and continued education. The appraisal regulations are intended to provide some transparency and act as an intermediary between lenders and borrowers. Appraisers are supposed to help the lending industry "play nice" with borrowers and establish benchmark valuations that lenders work with in establishing loan terms. The leading lenders (Wells Fargo, Bank of America, Comerica, etc.) order millions of appraisals yearly and around 76,000 appraisers (declining each year) prepare those reports. Is the appraised value always right? How can a homeowner help the appraiser come to a more accurate value? Take the advice in the previous discussion: you have a home that is well-maintained, energy efficient and have added "value enhanced" improvements that make your home more valuable than the typical home in the neighborhood. Both the lender and appraiser need to know this. Provide them with knowledge on why your home is more valuable before they start their processes.

When getting an appraisal on your commercial property, whether ordered from you or your lender, provide detailed income and expenses. On underperforming properties, show a business plan and budget to reflect a turn-around. If multi-tenant, run a discounted cash flow analysis and help the appraiser understand where you are taking the property. On conversions, get third party support for renovation. Broker letters supporting increased rents and occupancies will almost always support your cause.

- **Debt and Liens:** The residential lending market is pegged at about $17,000,000,000,000, more than the U.S. Treasury. The commercial lending market is reported to be around $11,000,000,000,000. Mortgage loans and other encumbrances affect the economics of real estate. Most people understand that the loan they get to purchase real estate becomes a mortgage instrument that they are required to pay off. Second mortgages occur when the equity in the real estate is pledged for additional debt and is secondary to the first mortgage. Tax liens, because of not paying real estate taxes or borrowing to pay real estate taxes, can take a priority above both first and second mortgages. Other liens can be imposed by court order, which further hold the real estate as collateral for the additional debt. Owner-occupied and investment purchasers need to review all debt and other liens to determine how they affect their purchases. Title companies review the 'chain of title' and insure against unknown claims. However, they typically do not insure against known claims.

- **Federal Tax Reduction Department:** For investment property owners, cost segregation is a vehicle for accelerating federal tax depreciation on improved property, providing for higher depreciation offsets sooner, like three, five and seven years. Cost segregation is an IRS-approved method for calculating costs of property components, segregating each building component's correct depreciation life, including short-life classifications. Accelerating (shorter) depreciation lowers or defers taxable income. Upon an investment property purchase, buyers should look to federal tax reduction companies to prepare these reports, which are then provided to accountants to "build into" tax returns.

- **Market Research Department:** Researching local property rental and occupancy statistics can be found on the Internet access of various real estate survey companies' databases of residential, apartment, office, retail, and industrial property characteristics. Subscribers have access to rent data, sale comps, and mortgages (maturing dates can be searched), tenant data and market reports. However, these subscriptions can cost thousands of dollars per month. Even the largest real estate firms use multiple search engines to get the totality of the data available in each market. Industry-leading brokerage firms, mortgage brokers, lenders and appraisers use multiple listing services like Costar, LoopNet, REIS and others. Nevertheless, processing the data takes a tremendous amount of money, time, and human resources. The industry is moving to data collectors where all public records become "enriched" through industry professional's use of the data and big data's ability to capture and store those "in the field" enhancements back into big databases. Appraiser's field inspections while preparing appraisal reports, crowd sourcing sales and rent comparables from lenders and broker's input allow the industry some transparency. However, nobody knows a property like the owner and once the big database collects that body of knowledge, real estate knowledge will then be truly transparent.

Does anyone think that the opening of Cuba to international trade and U.S. tourism will not have a measurable and long-term adverse effect on tourism in other Caribbean vacation spots? Strategic locations in Cuba are about to be developed with the leading hotel-branded resorts to which Americans and others will flock. Astute Canadians have been investing in the Cuban market for over a decade and are poised for substantial price appreciation. The Cuba labor market has a high literacy rate and low cost basis, making it an ideal resort vacation market.

Cuba's entry into the vacation market should adversely affect higher-priced vacation markets throughout the Caribbean and Latin America. Did the U.S. government consider these factors in their policy decisions? Should you consider a real estate investment in that market? Many savvy investors are going to make money on the "buy" side of this equation and benefit from a Cuba with a current "low volume" resort market that is going to stabilize over the next decade to one of the leading resort and vacation lifestyles in the world.

While the commercial and residential mortgage markets are massive economic stabilizers, in times of flux, uncertainties affect all aspects of quality of life and economics.

Cycles occur in most everyday walks-of-life: weather, relationships, raising children, and yes, the economy. So how does Big Data help us determine where we are in real estate cycles? Texas A&M Real Estate Research Center found that five key economic variables emerged as leading indicators to estimate residential construction cycles:

1. Housing starts;
2. Residential contract values;
3. Residential building permits;
4. The home mortgage rates; and
5. Unique factors affecting the local market for Texas and West Texas Intermediate (WTI) crude oil price.

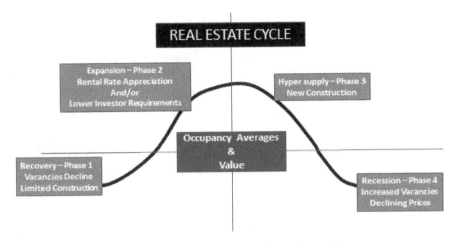

REAL ESTATE CYCLE

Expansion – Phase 2
Rental Rate Appreciation
And/or
Lower Investor Requirements

Hyper supply – Phase 3
New Construction

Occupancy Averages
&
Value

Recovery – Phase 1
Vacancies Decline
Limited Construction

Recession – Phase 4
Increased Vacancies
Declining Prices

Housing starts can be easily searched and tracked. These starts are so important to the U.S. economy that the U.S. Census (www.census.gov/construction/nrc/) is a leader in tracking this economic driver. Bloomberg, New York Times and Reuters regularly publish the data in leading news articles. Building permits on new homes can provide an early indicator of housing starts, but not all permits result in a home being constructed. There are many instances when the building permit is issued, but the construction of the home is not started due to the inability to get financing, or the inability to procure a buyer or occupant for the home.

What about construction trends? The industry's leading association, the National Association of Homebuilders, has yet to fully employ a national database of new home construction and trends. Days on market, ratio of listings to home sales over a particular period, and list price to home price ratio tend to be excellent gauges of the health of the regional home market.

But that data, aggregated into a single source, is impossible to find. The amount of time it takes to assemble and analyze all of the data, you might as well become an appraiser. And they even missed foreseeing the 2007 real estate downfall. That is why cycles occur, the inability to gauge the economics of the future; demand fever to "get into a market that is going up" and, government and lending policies that exacerbate a normalized market all play into the magnitude of the market variance.

Residential contract values are a little harder to track. McGraw Hill is a leader in publishing residential contract values. Permit values sometimes include contract values and can be found at the local city or county building permit offices. Local city or county building permit offices also provide residential building permit volumes. Again, the U.S. Census provides permit volumes at a regional and national level. Build Fax is a unique online service that connects almost every permit office in the country to a search engine.

One of the easiest factors to monitor is interest rates. Low interest rates provide incentive to borrowers to borrow. If the real estate market is appreciating, then investors have the most favorable economics. Conversely, high interest rates cause borrowers to be more conservative. They borrow less and have contracted "positive leverage."

U.S. lending practices have not been designed to fluctuate in cycles where real estate prices change quickly. Houston, Texas, could have a flat or even depreciating house pricing trend due to sub-$50 per barrel oil, while simultaneously Miami, Florida, has a 2% monthly appreciation due to international buyers enhancing the demand. Interest rates on home loans are typically a national established rate, but should have more variance when considering local market socio-economics.

When many Californians saw their home values double from 2000 to 2007, they used home equity loans (borrowed against their home's equity) to buy homes in Costa Rica. Home loans to foreign purchasers are rare in that country, so using cash from a home equity line where their $2,000,000 house appreciated $400,000 in four years seemed like a great investment. However, when house prices fell, the markets in both California and Costa Rica collapsed. Home equity loan rates are at levels above first mortgages, however when buyers use the equity to purchase a Costa Rican beachside bungalow, does the interest rate commensurate with the risk?

Let us now discuss some historical factors that helped lead the county into the last recession. Bill Clinton's presidency promoted the opportunity for everyone living in America to own a home, even if they were not a U.S. citizen or had the legal right to be in the country. The following factors did lead to massive foreclosures across the country and the inability for predictive analytics to help foresee this event was a big problem.

- Not having to show a driver's license,

- Not having to prove income levels, and

- Not having have to prove citizenship

Surely, other factors can help us see regional economic health. On both the national and regional basis, employment trends tend to be a huge bellwether of economic health. Increasing unemployment can show markets where flat or depreciating home prices may soon come. What happens if those not working tend be people in the lower economic strata? The contracting social group may be renters or live in communal housing, therefore not affecting home pricing.

In January 2015, the three leading economists in Houston, Texas, presented their 2015 projections at different events, suggesting that new job growth would be in the 50,000 to 60,000 range. By June 2015, all three revised their estimate to 15,000 to 25,000. The economy only created 20,700 jobs, and what was worse, most were entry level and service employment, not the $300,000+ oil engineer positions previously seen. An investor or homeowner relying on the projections made in January 2015 may have continued on their buying trend, but certainly not after June.

And what about Detroit, whose reputation in the housing markets downfall has been well played in the national media for years? While the economics of the housing market were primarily unemployment driven, the age of the housing stock, migration of middle to upper income households to certain parts of the city and an ineffective local government caused declining real estate trends to not only accelerate, but also increase in severity.

Then why would an investor purchase over 100 homes in Detroit, given the media's reporting of the negativity in the real estate market? Is it just contrarian investment, i.e., purchasing in a market that is depreciating and selling in a market that is appreciating in price? Well, there are fewer buyers using contrarian real estate investment strategies than those following the "sheep flock" mentality. The "piling" on of buyers in appreciating markets exacerbates the appreciation. In this century, new cities like Phoenix and Scottsdale have seen huge high and low cyclical price swings. At one time in the pre-2007 economy, speculators made up 22% of new home purchases in newly-built subdivisions. When the market stagnated, investors or lenders with foreclosed properties sold at any price and prices fell fast and far.

Except for those few shown in "The Big Short," few of the smartest bankers, economists and fortune tellers foresaw the last recession, certainly not to the level of economic collapse that actually occurred. Since 2008, data and particularly filtered real estate data has become very valuable. Hence, the impressive value multipliers put on real estate data companies. With the ability to purchase a terabyte of data storage for $60 and keep the phone sized storage in your pocket, every tech geek looking to change the industry is capable of making some contribution to the new technology age.

So look to numerous data sources to help in solving problems and enhance your decision making processes. Knowing a market requires both physical inspections and technology application proficiency. Further, buying multiple real estate assets to build wealth is not like cost averaging in the stock market. Look for trends and unique property outliers where the buy side of the equation can give you an edge.

TECHNOLOGY – THE GAME CHANGER

We will need to look at big data history, types of data and current uses of big data in technology applications in order to establish a knowledge based foundation that can help future entrepreneurs and programmers to formulate next generation technologies.

Definition of Big Data

There are numerous definitions for big data; numerous enough that they may qualify as big data. The writer prefers the following simple definition: Data combined from multiple sources for the purposes of gaining insights not available from the individual data sets to allow faster and better decision-making.

This definition does not address the petabytes of information. The speed of accessing data to make decisions is important. The three V's are also often included in definitions of big data: 1) volume, 2) velocity and 3) variety.

Regarding volume, there is consensus that more data is better. If in doubt and data is available, grab it. The costs of data storage are low and dropping annually. More data beats better algorithms because of correlations that could not be found in smaller data sets. The velocity of making data available exponentially increases the ability to make real-time decisions rather than decisions made 30 to 90 days after the fact. Have you ever reviewed a profit and loss statement to discover a large negative expense variance, only to realize that when you discovered the problem it had been occurring for months? Variety of data is the magic elixir that allows both straightforward reviews of graphs and advanced analytics to gain insights that have been intuitive.

Historical Perspective

In the third century BC, the Library of Alexandria was believed to house the sum of human knowledge. Today, there is enough information in the world to give every person alive 320 times as much of it as historians think was stored in Alexandria's entire collection -- an estimated 1,200 Exabyte's worth. Real estate contracts have seen little change in the last couple hundred years. Brokers want to be paid, hence the homeowner contracts for their services. Most states require written documentation of a real estate ownership transfer, hence purchase and closing contracts. Lastly, buyers want to know they own the real estate, hence title policy and insurance contracts.

Nevertheless, the Internet was a "game-changer" for the real estate transaction world. Rather than driving neighborhood streets, calling brokerage offices and looking at individual websites to see what listings are available, a prospective buyer can now look at thousands of homes in an hour with just a cell phone, tablet, and computer.

A survey in the 1990's indicated prospective homeowners would view at least 12 websites and visits up to nine homes prior to making a purchase decision. Now we can look into the interior of homes from thousands of miles away, even taking virtual reality views of proposed homes. Websites have even become less important, as computer applications tend to drive reoccurring visits. These applications provide client servicing features that not only assist buyers in finding a home, but also the logistics relative to the move and services available once in the home.

Technology adaption scales quicker today than ever in the past. The cell phone scaled to almost every person in the U.S., while it took 75+- years to get 90% television coverage. Applications and programs can scale as fast as a YouTube video of a cat playing with yarn. Facebook scaled to almost 150 million users in less than four years and Twitter to 54 million in the same time span, as millennials embrace technology like no other generation before. However, the banking industry has not yet fully employed millennials, as 60+ year old executives drive business plans from experience, rather than evaluating real time trends. Businesses focusing on technology-driven applications need to understand this client group, as they can enhance a company's revenue faster than any previous generation.

One thing that has not changed in 100 years in the housing market: the husband typically makes the decision on the pricing range and the wife typically makes the final decision of the few qualified home options.

Let us look at big data and how it is used in the real estate world.

Types of Data – Structured versus Unstructured

Structured data is typically in tables with defined field names. In big data collection, normalizing the data structure is a key to having data that can then be extracted for multiple applications. When the data fields are normalized across multiple data collection points, the data can then be used in processes and applications. Merely having massive data in different formats is not reflective of a platform that can be easily scaled. Knowing which data fields are important provides the base table structures for normalization.

Examples of structured data include: RFID logs, search indexes, shopping records from "best customer clubs" at supermarkets, readings from sensors, GPS signals from cell phones showing who is calling whom, GPS in cars to allow insurance companies to track speed and rate of braking by their insured for use in pricing, rides Uber drivers have given passengers is shared with the US government, criminal records, and toll-booth readings. Marital status, number of children at home, first new child at home, number of children versus number of bathrooms, and when last child leaves home (empty nest) are events that could trigger a change in home ownership. The date mortgage was originated, mortgage balance versus home value, and property tax loans are important factors

Unstructured data is not organized in a table or Excel format. It includes photos, video, social media posts such as Facebook and Twitter, text documents, data in reports such as appraisal reports that can't easily be retrieved. Forrester Research estimates that organizations effectively utilize less than five percent of their available data. The Internet is the ultimate source of unstructured big data.

Big data can be assembled from numerous sources:

- Computers in autos, airplanes and other machines monitor not only the machines' performance and when repairs are needed; they also take readings on the people using them. How fast they are going, where they are going, even what they are saying can be recorded.

- Computers in the home can now monitor electricity consumption, homeowner traits, and video feeds to record the status of the home. This data can be fed back through huge power grids so utility companies can monitor and manage peak demand and when shortages may occur.

- While historically public company data was available to the masses, now thousands of companies monitor and evaluate even private companies' data.

- Government data like sales taxes can be used to project revenue for private companies.

- Search engines like Google provide thousands and even millions of potential data points when searching companies, individuals, or topics.

Big Data Will Create Disruptive Change

Do you remember what happened as computers, fax machines, cell phones and smart phones each became available? Each had a transformative impact on the economy and lives of people. The impact of big data will dwarf the impact of any of these previous changes. Big Data will be the single most important change in management since the industrial revolution. It will create opportunities for riches for some existing companies and it will destroy companies who do not evolve. This may seem to be a bold and unsubstantiated statement. It is clear to us that the change will be revolutionary, after having implemented big data into the operations of our company.

Volume of Data Doubling Every Two Years

Moore's Law, named after Gordon Moore, one of the founders of Intel, estimated that the power of semiconductor chips would double every two years. The same is now occurring with data due to a change in the number of devices that measure and transmit it. O'Connor's Law states that the volumes of data available will double every two years.

Steps in Deciding How to Start Using Big Data

Utilizing big data is a step-by-step process. One does not go from hard copy documents to making most decisions using big data in a month. Implementation takes insight, planning, and execution. Big data should be used to compile information needed to make material decisions. These can include target market niches, the most productive prospects for marketing and sales, operations, logistics, manufacturing, and deciding which business sectors should be abandoned. While more is better to a data geek, for a business person the first step is to consider the most pressing strategic and tactical questions for the business for which information is needed. Determining the most critical business decision for which data is available or can be obtained is a good starting point for implementing Big Data.

Implementing Big Data

There are sophisticated computer programs that can perform amazing statistical analysis. However, businesses need data presented in a simpler form that is easily accessible for those of us who are not programmers. Relatively new programs allow generating analysis, graphical displays, and tables of data for computer novices. These programs are facilitating the revolution of businesses using big data. Programs like DOMO and Tableau allow companies to generate dashboards linked to real-time data such as production, quality control, sales, sales pipeline, revenue, and expenses, and variances for each of these items. Historically, income and expense data is reported 10 to 30 days after the end of the month. Functions of big data can be to assist in marketing, production, distribution, finance, supply chain or any other part of the business by showing the real-time. Most of this data can be available real-time or within a day, allowing management to make strategic modifications quickly.

Processing Data

We are all familiar with the phrase "garbage in generates garbage out." What is not implicit is that data processing and cleansing separate quality data from garbage. Most data collectors extract public and/or private data through web applications (Pokémon Go), records (courthouses are great data depositories) and documents, in-person data collection (copy data to disk or zip drives or even film code, scans and pictures of records and documents), data feeds (typically API or excel/xml type file) and through manual data extraction (person keying in the data into a computer).

After data is gathered, cleansing the data to eliminate typos, anomalies and other errors is an essential step to benefiting from big data. The path toward generating structured data instead of unstructured data can reasonably be expected to require years since it involves changes in behavior.

But why do most residential and commercial brokerage websites look the same? They provide a search engine that allows visitors to queue homes they find interesting and look at the physical characteristics and aesthetics of the home. What about the psychology of home purchasing? Moreover, what about the psychographic responses to a new homeowner to their surroundings? Spatial and color dynamics are important, as is the color of the carpet. Now overlay the ability to walk to coffee shops, walk the dog, biking trails, access to open space areas; we get to really know the area before making the purchase.

Real estate advisory and database companies have the highest price/earnings ratio and market cap per employee; low number of employees per company; positive returns on assets, equity and high operating margins. Types of companies currently subscribing to the data in real estate databases are:

1. Leading investment real estate brokerage service companies;

2. The world's leading media and communications companies;

3. Regional real estate brokers, who also invest in land and developing;

4. Leading office owners and property managers;

5. Largest private apartment brokerage firms in the nation;

6. Largest cities in the U.S.;

7. Largest title companies in the state and U.S.;

8. Largest retail property owners in the state and U.S.;

9. One of the largest school districts in the state;

10. Largest pest control companies in the state and U.S.;

11. Firm managing over 50,000 multi-family units/1M SF commercial;

12. Local and regional appraisal companies;

13. Real estate services and investment brokerage firm with offices in 180 cities and 30 countries.

Search results for property sales and rents are a standard feature of big data. Overlays with mortgage and contact data enrich the data, making each data record more valuable. Then adding detailed contact data allows users to scale their business, as they reach out to people in businesses, real estate buyers/owners and sellers/listings to enhance business growth. Following is an example of data provided through www.enricheddata.com.

Industrial Lease Data – Houston, Texas

Source: www.enricheddata.com

Real estate data can include, but is not limited to, details on the broker, buyer, seller, lender, management company, tenant (owner occupied, tenants and/or vacant), physical and economic characteristics. Rent comparables are single and multi-tenant buildings with details on owner, management company, broker, tenant, physical, and economic characteristics. The data collections allow marketing to business leads and provides the data to conduct broker price opinions and appraisals. Millions of companies provide services to homeowners and commercial building owners.

Apartment Mortgages in Houston Coming Due in 12 Months

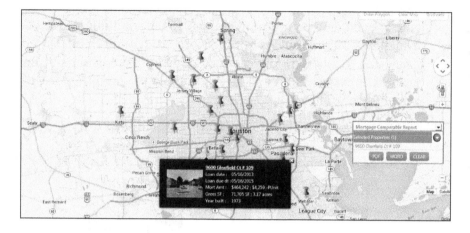

Source: www.enricheddata.com

Putting sales (deed data) and deeds of trust (mortgages) data, coupled with industry professionals' input over base public record data, into a manageable and searchable database with rent, sales and tenant data, crowd sourcing data from appraisers and lenders provides for a **"Living Network of Real Estate Professionals and Real Estate Information."** That information, correctly processed, allows businesses to lead the industry in their respective fields!

How Do You Access Big Data

Technical professionals integrate routines, protocols, and tools for building software and applications under Application Programming Interface (API), Virtual Private Network (VPN) or Public Access to the database, with an API to be the preferred strategy.

Why An API Strategy?

- Software applications are numerous and few have been connected to databases. Connecting data to software applications through an API allows a digital transformation, i.e., a universal software connector.

- APIs can be quickly employed without affecting the database or the application.

- Developers proficient in difference ecosystems can connect through APIs.

- REST (Representational State Transfer) APIs easily stage the data for universal connectivity to applications.
- APIs employ security protocols, including password protections.
- APIs provide security mechanisms to manage output and input of data.
- Businesses use API implementation for flexibility in small scale projects.

A client can access national real estate information and related people contact database records contained in a Structured Query Language (SQL) database. SQL is used to communicate with a database. Even IBM is allowing hundreds of businesses to access the power of Watson through API access. According to ANSI (American National Standards Institute), an API is the standard language for relational database management systems. Companies, like Rackspace, provide hosting security in climate-controlled environments with a portfolio of services.

Database integrity should cover three critical security areas:

1. Physical Security;

2. Operational Security; and

3. System Security.

Physical security provides for card, fingerprint, and facial feature requirements.

- Access to select employees that are screened and designated as technicians.
- 24-hour personal security.

Operational security monitors and limits access to confidential information.

- Encrypted data transmission.
- Destruction of customer data.
- Audit trail.

System security with hardened operating systems (OS) requires periodic patching.

- Monitoring and upgrading fire-wall systems to block unauthorized access.

- Redundant back-up systems to protect data integrity.

- Virtual private network to prevent unauthorized access.

- Intrusion detective devices.

API writers and programmers need to have extensive backgrounds in programming and technical writing; with extensive programming background in the .NET Framework under "managed code." .Net is a software framework developed by Microsoft that runs on Microsoft Windows and includes a large class library known as Framework Class Library (FCL) and provides language interoperability across several programming languages. Programs written for .NET Framework execute in a software environment (as contrasted to hardware environment) known as Common Language Runtime (CLR), an application virtual machine that provides services such as security, memory management, and exception handling.

Programmers produce proprietary software by combining a known source code with .NET Framework and other libraries to produce proprietary software applications that lead "Best in Business" class companies. An effective API document is written by professionals working on numerous company and application environments who can relate the strength of the database to the software applications and the various components construct the overall purpose of the intended client programs.

The Web API is defined as "An interface to a software component that can be invoked at a distance over a communications network using standards based technologies." It comprises of REST endpoints are HTTP requests an application can make to read or write a digital resource.

1. The API will need to authenticate:

   a. Developers,

   b. Applications, and

   c. End-users.

2. API security is employed through an authentication protocol.

3. API Manager will provision rules established in the Statement of Work Agreement and regulate API usage and consumption.

Data receivers:

1. Expose valuable data resources;

2. Allow API requests to return filtered data using query parameters;

3. Use query parameters for advanced filtering, sorting & searching; and

4. Use HTTPS and SSL everywhere, no exceptions.

A RESTful API can expose the data to other companies that will download the data for processing in their business and applications. An example is Enriched Data's national mortgage data in the form of OData. This API can be accessed in cloud with proper security key, so that end user can receive the needed data. Sample fields exposed in an API could include:

Field Name	Description
AccountID:	Property Account number
Property_Street_Number	Property Street number
Property_Street_Name:	Property Street Name
Property_County:	Property County
Property_State:	Property State
Property_Zip:	Property Zip
Metro:	Property Metro
Property_Type:	Property Major Type
Borrower_Or_Mortgagor_Name:	Borrower name
Borrower_Contact_Name:	Borrower contact person name
Title:	Borrower contact person title
Borrower_Address:	Borrower Address (Street number, Street Name)
Borrower_City:	Borrower City
Borrower_State:	Borrower State
Borrower_Zip_Code:	Borrower Zip Code
Borrower_Phone_1:	Borrower - Primary Contact Number

Borower_Phone_1_Type:	Borrower – Primary Contact Number Type (Ex: Office)
Borrower_Email:	Borrower – Email Id
Borrower_LinkedIn_Link:	Borrower Linked in Link
Borrower_Website:	Borrower Website

Now we can discuss other methods of accessing big data.

Intranet

Intranet definition is: a computer network with restricted access, as within a company, that uses software and protocols developed for the Internet. Larger companies allow employees and clients to access proprietary applications and data through an intranet application.

Virtual Private Network (VPN)

VPN, or virtual private network, is a network that is constructed by using the Internet to connect to Enriched Data's private network. Companies can implement a number of systems that enable them to use the Internet and access programs as the medium for transporting data. These systems use encryption and other security mechanisms to ensure that only authorized users can access the network and that the data cannot be intercepted.

The first step to security is a firewall requiring the remote user to establish an authenticated connection.

A company can manage the infrastructure while another provides hosting, architecture advice and guidance, code development assistance, and launch managers for hosted servers. Database records can be made directly available. In most cases, a Table Structure will be created to allow data population for the specific business platform.

Contact Management

With increased business comes increased client contact. And the old days of closing dinners and golf outings are not important to the new generation. They want to work enough to maximize their "me" and social time. So what does the 62 year-old mortgage banker need to do? Well, they need to do what the millennials do, use programs to help manage their contacts. While Sales Force is one of the most well-known client relationship management (CRM) software programs, there are others, e.g., Smart Sheets, Zoho, Netsuite, Oncontact and Act.

For many companies, loading contact data into client relationship management (CRM) systems is key to monitor, manage, and increase productivity levels of their professionals. A CRM system allows management to view their professional's calling, emailing and business "pipeline," and producers to manage client interaction. Using a CRM system within an established business platform that implements strategies and technologies to manage and analyze custom interactions and data throughout the customer life cycle, will help improve business performance. Customer retention along with driving new business to the platform allows companies to grow strategically.

Sales pipeline reports help companies capture leads and customer data more accurately and convert leads to prospects and eventually more sales. Efficiencies can be obtained by measuring which successful marketing and sales campaigns drive the most business, and then scale those successes across the entire business platform. Prospects want to know there is a value proposition to motivate them to be clients. They want to be able to process the data provided quickly and effectively. And adding some new knowledge indicators allows them to be ahead of their competition. When homeowners become "empty nesters" could be particularly important to a real estate agent. It provides a life event when a family may want to downsize their home, resulting in both a sell and buy opportunity. And what about a company's employees who benefit from a recent stock option distribution? Could that monetization allow a family to be move-up buyers?

Collecting behavioral data on people is an important factor in big data processing. **But that data needs to be processed in such a way that it becomes an enhancement to basic real estate economics; occupancy, rental rates, sale prices, operating expenses and capitalization rates.**

While emails have become the most-used intermediary between business professionals, marketing through emails rarely results in a 3%+ open rate (the percentage of time the receiver opens the email and hopefully reads it). Most email marketing results in the receiver moving it to the trash bin, with automated tools to initiate never having to receive an email from that sender again. CRM systems can tract "tag" lines that are more successful than others. Changing up the message till you get a tag line is a key. What is the best introductory line when cold calling new prospects? What are factors that make existing clients renew their subscriptions?

Predetermined contact and property data fields can be uploaded into various CRM systems to help professionals manage multiple leads and business opportunities through the sales cycle (lead, prospect, and then client or lost). An example of a few well known CRM systems are:

1. Base;
2. Smart Sheets;
3. Act Online;
3. Sales Force;
4. Goldkey;
5. Outlook; and
6. There are over 50 more known applications.

Now that we can keep track of the owners, buyers, sellers and industry professionals, it is important to discuss needed data points that allow big real estate data to be easily filtered.

Land Use Codes (LUC)

The following discussion will outline Land Use Codes (LUC) and select property types, as adopted by the Appraisal Institute. It is important for real estate data processors, residential and commercial investors to understand these categories in order to standard big data affecting real estate.

However, not all counties in the U.S. provide LUC codes; as a result, photos of the properties are needed in order for a data analyst to apply the most likely LUC code based on the visual inspection. While we will not go through all 110+ land use types, look to specialty property types to become an expert and differentiate yourself in the market.

- Aquaculture: A facility for growing fish, shellfish, and other marine life in controlled conditions for the production of food. a.k.a. fish farms. Commonly grown marine life includes but is not limited to: many types of fish, oysters, shrimp, crabs, lobster, and seaweed.

- Greenhouse / Nursery: A facility designed for the growing or producing plants, trees, or vegetables under climatically controlled conditions, including hydroponics. Typically not a retail facility, e.g., commercial and retail Garden Center

- Assembly or Meeting Place: Facilities for public or private meetings. Note, annual revenue from private and semi-private clubs in the U.S. exceeds the movie industry!

  o Club/Lodge: A place where members of an organized social group gather for various activities. May have a small kitchen and bar area where beverages are served.

  o Reception and Banquet Hall: Open floor plan assembly hall with no fixed seating and an adjoining commercial kitchen capable of meeting the food preparation needs of a wedding reception or other type of large dinner event.

  o Religious Facility: A building or group of buildings devoted to religious practices or housing for the clergy.

  o Kiosk: Typically less than 800 sq.ft. selling fast-moving items found in traditional convenience stores such as tobacco, beverages, snacks, and confectionaries.

- Day Care Facility: A facility intended to care for pre-school children, elderly adults, or individuals with special needs during the day.

  o Child: Daytime care center for pre-school children.

  o Adult: Daytime care center for elderly adults.

  o Other Day Care: Daytime care center for individuals with special needs.

- Tavern, Bar, Nightclub, Micro-Brewery: Commercial establishments oriented around the sale, and on-site consumption of alcoholic beverages.

- Healthcare: Facilities for public or private, acute or chronic, health and medical services.

    o Clinical Laboratory: A clinical testing center or laboratory, e.g., blood testing, serum lab, etc.

    o Rehabilitation Center: A recovery facility oriented toward the long-term treatment and rehabilitation of sick or injured persons so they can function in society. Rehabilitation follows stabilization of any acute medical conditions.

    o Urgent Care Center: An outpatient clinic where ill or injured persons can receive a wide range of smaller medical services with or without an appointment; a.k.a. immediate-care facility

- Housing: Property as a place to live. A dwelling unit is a single-housing unit occupied by one or more related or unrelated people living together as a social group.

    o Assisted Living: Designed for elderly persons or individuals with debilitating diseases who do need assistance with activities of daily living (ADL) but do not require continuous skilled nursing care. Essentially an apartment with additional services like cooking, housecleaning, or minor nursing care. May be in a separate wing or floor of a congregate residence, though licensure requirements for this type facility are generally more stringent than for congregate units.

    o Congregate and Independent Living: Essentially an apartment without medical services. Designed for the elderly who pay for some services like housekeeping, transportation, & meals on a monthly basis, but require little, if any, assistance with daily living activities like eating, dressing, and bathing. Residents may or may not receive health care provided by on-site staff or external agency. May also be a retirement community designed to attract young retirees by emphasizing outdoor recreational activities. il

- o Continuing-Care Retirement Community: A facility designed, staffed, & equipped to accommodate elderly who do not need hospital care, but require skilled nursing care, other medical services, and assistance with daily living activities. Some CCRC properties feature a combination of congregate and independent living units, assisted living beds, and skilled nursing beds. Other facilities offer just congregate and independent units and skilled nursing beds.

- o Skilled Nursing Facility: Includes all licensed nursing beds. Skilled nursing facilities (SNF) are state-licensed nursing homes, which provide around-the-clock care for convalescent patients, a level of care just below acute hospital care.

- o Student: Multiple-unit housing with specialized features for students.

- o Dormitory: A single building containing multiple sleeping quarters. Typical features include a central food preparation area, shared dining room, and communal lavatories.

- o Fraternity and Sorority: A dwelling owned, maintained and inhabited by members of a specific group or affiliation. Common features include a large food preparation area, large dining area, and sometimes a large meeting room. Lavatories are often communal.

- Lodging and Hospitality: Property designed primarily to serve short or medium-term overnight stays in a commercial establishment.

  - o All Suites: Guest rooms with a bedroom area apart from a living or sitting area.

  - o Bed and Breakfast: A house, generally an older renovated residence, where lodging and breakfast are provided to paying guests. A portion of the guest rooms often require the use of communal restrooms.

  - o Casino Hotel: A lodging facility combined with a full casino gaming facility.

o Convention Hotel: Hotels designed to accommodate large groups and functions. They provide facilities such as one or more large ballrooms with breakout areas for meetings and conferences, exhibit space for trade shows, sample and display rooms for sales meetings, extensive restaurant and lounge capacity, and some recreational amenities found in commercial hotels. The key component is meeting space, which should amount to at least 30 square feet per guestroom. They are sometimes located next to convention centers.

o Economy Hotel and Motel: A facility that typically features exterior lodging-room access, minimal or no recreational facilities, and few, if any, conveniences.

o Extended Stay: A hotel designed for travelers who must stay in an area for a prolonged period, typically seven or more days. Amenities offered create a more home-like environment than a standard hotel. Guestrooms often have a full, eat-in kitchen with separate sleeping and living areas. Food and beverage services are limited. This type hotel is a cross between an apartment and an all-suite hotel.

o Full Service: A facility that offers a wide array of services including but not limited to: room service, valet, concierge, transportation, tour services, barber shop, beauty salon, bellhop service, laundry service, full liquor service in a lounge, restaurant, turndown service, morning newspaper, fitness center, swimming pool, banquet hall, and meeting space, etc.

o Limited Service: Typical features include interior lodging-room access, some recreational and exercise facilities, and some conveniences. May offer limited food and liquor service.

o Luxury: A full-service hotel that features sumptuous physical surroundings and services. Much of the extravagance is considered nonessential but conducive to pleasure and comfort. Also known as five-star hotel.

- o Resort and Spa: A hotel typically situated in a scenic area that either provides or is near activities that attract leisure travelers. Nearby recreation may include: swimming, tennis, golf, boating, skiing, ice skating, riding, hiking, and sightseeing. Services offered may include: restaurant, lounge, entertainment, fitness center, concierge, valet service, local transportation, tour services, and a limited amount of meeting and banquet space. The level of occupancy is often seasonal.

- Recreation: Properties where people congregate, often in large numbers, for sports related, entertainment, or recreational activities.

  - o Amusement Facility: A recreation center oriented around game activities and / or thrill rides.

  - o Amusement and Theme Park: A permanently located, commercially-operated park offering various forms of entertainment such as arcade games, carousels, roller coasters, and performers as well as food, drink, and souvenirs. Differs from circuses, carnivals, and fairs which typically travel. Theme parks are specialty amusement parks designed to evoke distant or imaginary locales and / or eras, such as the Wild West, an African safari, or medieval Europe.

  - o Aquatic Facility and Swimming Pool: A facility with indoor and / or outdoor pools for public swimming. They exclude waterslide facilities which are classified separately.

  - o Arcade: A commercial establishment featuring rows of coin-operated games.

  - o Bowling Alley: A commercial facility designed to accommodate the sport of bowling. The building includes special equipment and design features such as a ball return, pin-setting equipment and bowling lanes with gutters.

o Go-Cart Track: Small-scale track that allows patrons to operate mini-race cars.

o Miniature Golf: A novelty version of golf played with a putter and ball on a miniature, artificial-turf course with obstacles such as bridges, tunnels, and small waterways.

o Waterslide Park: Recreation center oriented around water slides, wave pools and other water-related activities.

o Casino and Gaming Facility: Free standing gambling parlor that does not offer lodging. Casino hotels are classified under Lodging.

o Cinema: A facility where motion pictures are shown

o Theater, Indoor, Single Screen: A public establishment that offers just one motion picture screen; usually located in an antiquated building.

o Theater, Indoor, Multiple Screen: A more modern, public facility for simultaneously projecting multiple motion pictures in separate rooms. May contain multiple motion picture formats like wide screen and 3D.

o Drive-in theater: Outdoor movie theater where the audience remains in their own cars to watch a motion picture. Typically consists of a large tract with individual sound speaker hookups that temporarily attach to the car. Limited small building to house a concession stand and restrooms.

o Equestrian Center: A facility for riding and showing horses. Facilities generally include stables, training pens, and access to riding trails. Higher-end centers will include a restaurant and club house and possibly a small arena for polo and riding exhibitions.

- Fitness, Courts, and Spa Facilities: An exercise and recreation property that includes fitness training, court sports, locker rooms, and/or spa facilities.
  - Court Facility: An exercise facility designed for competitive activities played on a court. Examples include tennis, racquetball, handball, squash, etc.
  - Health and Fitness Center, Sports Club and Gym: An exercise facility featuring an assortment of weight-resistance training, aerobic activities, and locker room with shower facilities. Category encompasses a wide range of facilities. Lower-end facilities may only provide weight-training equipment while upper-end facilities may include court sports, swimming pools, classes, and spa treatments.
  - Rock Climbing: A fitness center characterized by a large, open space and ceiling height of 30 or more feet and a small portion of office space. May or may not include locker rooms.
  - Spa Resort: A relaxation, rejuvenation, recreation hotel destination. Modern spas provide therapeutic treatments and exercise, and are usually located in scenic areas that may also include recreational activities such as golf, tennis, or skiing.
  - Other Fitness & Court Facilities: All other fitness, courts, and spa facilities not classified otherwise.
- Golf Related: A property oriented towards the sport of golf.
  - Driving Range: Golf practice facility that typically consists of a driving and putting practice area.
  - Golf Course Club: A facility for playing the game of golf. Improvements typically include specific design, grading, landscaping, irrigation system, clubhouse with food and beverage service, and storage; may be a public or private country club.
  - Golf Resort: An upscale destination oriented around a golf course; may have other club facilities available.

- o Other Golf: All other golf-related facilities not classified otherwise.

- Racetrack: A venue designed to meet the needs of competitive racing. Minimum improvements typically include spectator stands lined around a raceway, food concessions, and lavatory facilities.

- Auto: A venue designed to meet the needs of competitive auto racing. At a minimum, improvements include spectator stands around a raceway, food concessions, and lavatory facilities.

- Dog: A venue designed to meet the needs of competitive dog racing. At a minimum, improvements include spectator stands around a raceway, food concessions, lavatory facilities, and betting cages.

- Horse: A venue designed to meet the needs of competitive horse racing. At a minimum, improvements include spectator stands around a raceway, food concessions, lavatory facilities, and betting cages.

- Other Racetrack: All other racetracks not classified otherwise.

- Shooting Range: A specialized facility designed for firearms or archery practice; may be indoor or outdoor.

- Skating Facility: A property designed to accommodate skating sports; includes both indoor and outdoor facilities. May include figure skating, curling, ice hockey, roller skating, skateboarding, and in-line-wheel skating.

- Ski Resort: A mountain or hillside recreation area oriented around snowboarding, downhill and / or cross-country skiing, and other winter sports.

- Sports Arena or Stadium: A large-scale venue designed to stage athletic competitions before large audiences.

- Indoor high-capacity arena: An enclosed arena designed for large-scale sporting and entertainment events.

- Outdoor high-capacity open-air arena: Arena designed for large-scale sporting and entertainment events.

- Theater and Performing Arts Facility: A building where theatrical performances are held. Audience seating areas typically rise away from the stage or screen on a slope or stepped incline to allow visibility for the entire audience or members.

- Auditorium Building: A large hall designed for a stage performance. Acoustical features include noise dampening walls that minimize noise reflection as well as a ceiling design that maximizes sound projection to the far reaches of the hall.

- Concert Hall and Arena: A large seating and sound-stage facility with better acoustics and seating accommodations than an auditorium.

- Outdoor Amphitheater: An outdoor concert sound stage that typically includes a band shell to project the performance toward audience seating.

- Death Related Facilities: Facilities that temporarily store or prepare corpses for burial or cremation. See Land, Cemetery or Mausoleum

  o Funeral Home: Funeral homes provide services to prepare corpses for final disposition. Services include one or more of the following: embalming to delay decomposition, displaying corpses in large open rooms for visitation by friends and family, cremation, and movement of a corpse to a gravesite or mausoleum.

  o Crematory: A crematory reduces the remains of corpses to ashes by intense heat.

  o Mortuary: Mortuaries store corpses awaiting identification, autopsy, or final disposition by burial or cremation.

  o Other Death Related : All other death related facilities not classified otherwise.

- Kennel: A facility designed for the short-term shelter, caring, and maintenance of animals, mostly cats and dogs.

- Marina: A water basin and adjacent dry land providing dockage and other services to pleasure and commercial water craft. Services provided include one or more of the following: fueling stations, docks, boat ramps, loading and unloading, restaurant and bar, repair and maintenance, convenience store, yacht club, and enclosed or outdoor water-craft storage.

- Movie Studio: A facility used in the production of motion pictures.

- Pier: A structure built on posts extending from land out over water. Common uses include a landing place for water pleasure craft, entertainment, eateries, fishing, and strolling.

- Outdoor Sign: The land and a vertical structure with a flat, vertical surface that displays a message; often for advertising.

- Veterinary Clinic: A facility designed and used for providing medical care to many kinds of animals.

- Watercraft Repair & Storage: A facility, not adjacent to water, that repairs, maintains, or stores water pleasure craft.

- Other Special Purpose: All other special-purpose facilities not classified otherwise

Database LUC codes with property records. Filter and map those preferences important to you. And for larger companies, bring a culture of like-minded professionals together who want solutions to the industries using these facilities.

What You Need To Know About Properties

Once the data points are standardized, data aggregation of the following data sets allows data processors to build filters to evaluate trends and meaningful comparisons across properties and time.

1. Commercial buildings and commercial land

- Tax roll data
- Sales information for the last 10 to 12 years
- Deeds of trust for last 10 to 12 years
- Detailed contact data for the borrower and signatory for deeds of trust maturing in future

- Detailed and carefully researched ownership contact information for owner contact person including multiple phone numbers, email address, Linked In, Fax #, Facebook
- Property characteristics (size, type of construction, land area, building area, grade of construction, building class, parking, type parking, etc)
- Tenants
- Property amenities
- Asking rental rate and occupancy
- Spaces for lease
- Ownership with contact data
- Owner's home address and psychographic profile
- Management with contact data
- Leasing with contact data
- Property images including photo, maps, flood map, facet map, etc.

2. Single family (houses, townhomes, coops, condos and lots)

- Tax roll data
- Detailed information on land parcel and characteristics
- Information on last sales including sales price
- QCLV – Fannie Mae information – quality, condition, location and view, as compiled by appraisers.
- Prior deeds of trust and current deed of trust, including maturity and interest rate when available
- Property characteristics such as information often found in the MLS
- Owner occupied or tenant
- Rental rate
- Ownership with detailed contact information for owner (phone, email, fax, Linked-In, Facebook, Twitter)
- Psychographic information on owner
- Property images such as photos, maps, flood map, facet map, etc.

Processing Real Estate Data to Get What You Want

"As I experience certain sensory input patterns my mental pathways become accustomed to them. The inputs eventually are anticipated and even 'missed' when absent."

Experienced participants in the real estate market have the same 'mental pathways' developed. Before Big Data, the challenge has been to build that knowledge in their brains and constantly monitor many different data sources for changes and trends. Here are examples of how Big Data, and Enricheddata.com can specifically aid two such 'niches.' There are over 1,000 data inputs in a typical residential or commercial appraisal. Data from public and private sources, which may be confidential, provide the information. What is needed for an appraisal:

- Market Reports – Market analysis of the specific property type on a macro and micro level is needed to determine the historical and projected trends for rental rates, occupancy, concessions, and proposed construction.

- Sale Comparables – Sales of similar properties are analyzed to determine the most probable value for the subject.

- Rental Comparables – Rents from other properties are used to determine the most probable rent for the subject.

- For Sale Listings – Comparable properties listed for sale in the market can be a great measure of demand and pricing.

Big data processed quickly and efficiently can assist appraisers to be more accurate and meet their client's expectations.

Real estate brokers, not only, must know all aspects of the property being marketed, but also, the market in which that property is situated and all competitive purchase and investment options available to prospective buyers. An internet search for "Texas Real Estate Data" returns 463,000,000 results.

- Enriched Data (www.enricheddata.com) incorporates, not only, 100,000,000+ searchable real estate records with links to public information, but also, compares and consolidates occupancy, rental rates, sales, mortgages, tenants, space availability, market reports on a metro and submarket basis, and contact information on over 2,000,000 owners, sellers, lenders, leasing and sales brokers, managers, and tenants in the marketplace. This site is probably the most comprehensive single source of data research with results that can be downloaded in a Word, PDF and/or Excel format. Broker price opinions and evaluations can be run on any property in minutes.

- No doubt, Texas A&M Real Estate Center, (http://recenter.tamu.edu/data/), is a leader in consolidating building permits, employment and unemployment, housing activity and affordability and population in historical charts and graphs. This is one of the few sources for rural land trends.

- Zillow, Inc. (NASDAQ: Z), operates a leading real estate and home-related marketplace on mobile and the Web, and has 50 million monthly unique users.

- The Texas Association of Realtors consolidates quarterly reports on home trends; reporting 53,937 single family homes sold in 1st Quarter of 2013, a 17% increase from 1st Quarter 2012.

Processing 190,000,000 mortgages recorded in the U.S. requires a team of over 1,000 data collectors at courthouses across the U.S. who still use microfiche, thousands of off-shore data analyst who digitize the data, and computer programmers who build sophisticated algorithms to deliver search results. Enhancing the results with search capabilities that are thorough and unique provides market clarity that previously was not available. But what does a mortgage banker really want to know? Out of 450 fields of information to process per property, which 20 for 40 fields are important to interpret for an increase in business?

A "bottom up" approach is traditionally what real estate professionals had been looking for. The first step is to acquire quality information on individual properties and the contacts (seller, owner, broker, lender, tenant, and management company) associated with that property. Then make it searchable through (www.enricheddata.com). Next, the ability to aggregate is a great way to assemble big data in the real estate marketplace. Appraisers, brokers, and other real estate professionals, as well as owners at the local level confirming and contribute property transaction information on a property by property basis. By getting that information into the data base it continually enhances the quality of the data on a granular and aggregate level.

A "top down" approach, targeting large companies who have thousands of clients, takes sophistication, relationships, and months and sometimes years to procure a contract. We recently completed one contract with the largest, "best in class" real estate technology company that took over two years to complete! Every day of negotiating, waiting and stressing was well worth it.

Not only does the processing of big data mean "Big Money," but also, those embracing its use will experience ease in processing documents, increase in market knowledge, and the ability to analyze historical trends to make assumptions on future trends.

A Comparative Analysis of the Valuation Research Assistant (VRA) to Automated Valuation Model (AVM) Performance

The purpose of modeling this validation exercise was to determine how accurate existing mass valuation models for mass appraisal are. There were two measures of accuracy.

1. To measure the performance of the Valuation Research Assistant (VRA) against well-established Automated Valuation Models (AVM), and

2. To explore the impact of model data on overall model performance, specifically, answering the question, "after adjusting for model input data, do the models perform differently?"

Through the industry-accepted practice of valuation model testing and the use of different types of benchmark values against which to compare the models, the VRA model was shown to demonstrate significantly improved comparative performance when using benchmark values to which the comparative models did not have access.

VRA proved to be an above-average performer when evaluated using all benchmarks where one or more of the other three valuation models may have had related data which provided an advantage. VRA's performance vs. the comparative models improved noticeably when evaluated using only the subset of benchmark data for which the comparative models had no, or very limited access to related data which might have provided an advantage to the comparative models.

The following defines and discusses the specific parameters, processes and outcomes of the testing and analysis that was completed in 2014 to achieve the aforementioned objectives.

In mortgage lending, it is common for models that render an estimated value of a residential property to be used for portfolio review, equity lending, quality control, marketing, and as a part of fraud detection programs.

Test Methodology

The evaluation of valuation model performance is based upon comparing the model's predicted value to a "benchmark" value. The benchmark value represents the best estimate of the property's true market value at a point in time. Historically, the ideal benchmark has been a recent sale price of a property established by a willing buyer and seller absent any duress indicated by situations like short-sale, impending foreclosure, or other unusual circumstance. In recent years, the increased use of multiple listing service (MLS) data, in some valuation models have weakened the recent sale price as an ideal benchmark. With MLS data, valuation models have some insight into the recent sale via the listing price of the benchmark property. To address this situation, the evaluation of the VRA model and the AVMs to which it is compared was based, in part, on the use of a full appraisal as one benchmark value. Typically, the transaction is a refinance or an equity loan or line of credit. With these transactions, there is no sale taking place and, therefore, no listing price. The analysis of VRA and the AVMs to which it is compared will include a breakdown by benchmark type: sale price or appraised value.

For this evaluation, only full form 1004 appraisals are used as benchmarks. Although a contract price may vary from the actual final sales price in virtually all cases; in this case the two values match exactly.

The base metric used to evaluate model performance is the percentage error (% error) and is calculated as:

$$\% \; Error = (Model \; Predicted \; Value - Benchmark \; Value) \, / \, Benchmark \; Value$$

With this, a positive error indicates that the model has overvalued the property and a negative value indicates that the model has undervalued the property.

Given that the primary source of modeling data is public record sales transactions which are recorded at the county; it is an accepted practice to evaluate model performance by county. Like most models, valuation models are comprised of data and analytics. The data can be considered the fuel or raw material of the model. The analytics is the mathematics and statistics which convert the data into a usable form. This becomes an important point because model performance is affected by both the data and the analytics. In order for a model to perform well it must have both good data and good analytics. If either is subpar, the output of the model will suffer.

Two types of benchmarks used in this analysis: 1) a contract price, and 2) a full appraisal. The use of the full appraisal mitigates the impact of MLS data by presenting transactions where no sales activity is occurring; therefore, no MLS data is present.

The 10% accuracy rate is defined as the percentage of the values applied to homes in a county which fell within 10% of the sale price or appraised value. An example would be 73.59% of all values concluded by this mass appraisal product fell within 10% of the home prices or appraised value for each home in the county. Hence, 26.41% of the concluded values fell outside of 10% of the sale price or appraised value. This metric has become a common metric by which to assess AVM performance.

Obviously, we are hoping for a fairly high percentage accuracy rate, because when industry participants purchase residential mortgage backed securities (RMBS) or big lenders what to evaluate their existing residential portfolio's value against its debt, accuracy is extremely important!

The test included 18,168 residential properties, but we will show you only a small percentage of the counties. Each property had a contract price or a full 1004 appraised value. Each of the four AVMs is built upon slightly different data sets and algorithms. One of the four makes moderate use of MLS data. The second AVM uses public record data and the third uses a proprietary data set.

10% ACCURACY RATE BY COUNTY

COUNTY, ST	HOME SALES	AVM 1 10% AR	AVM 2 10% AR	AVM 3 10% AR	AVM 4 10% AR
MARICOPA, AZ	337	57.27%	73.59%	73.00%	61.42%
LOS ANGELES, CA	295	62.71%	63.05%	74.92%	53.90%
CLARK, NV	146	54.11%	84.25%	73.97%	67.81%
RIVERSIDE, CA	130	56.92%	76.92%	73.85%	63.08%
COOK, IL	124	41.13%	63.71%	68.55%	32.26%
SACRAMENTO, CA	119	46.22%	72.27%	61.34%	65.55%
BROWARD, FL	114	45.61%	72.81%	67.54%	50.00%
SAN DIEGO, CA	109	57.80%	71.56%	81.65%	60.55%
MONTGOMERY, OH	99	42.42%	53.54%	79.80%	19.19%
SANTA CLARA, CA	92	58.70%	63.04%	76.09%	58.70%
HARRIS, TX	86	54.65%	79.07%	79.07%	17.44%
OAKLAND, MI	55	38.18%	74.55%	76.36%	41.82%
DALLAS, TX	51	52.94%	68.63%	82.35%	7.84%
PALM BEACH, FL	51	43.14%	84.31%	70.59%	43.14%
ORANGE, FL	48	45.83%	70.83%	72.92%	56.25%
CONTRA COSTA, CA	47	72.34%	80.85%	68.09%	70.21%

For data where a full appraisal was the benchmark, AVM 4 has the highest 10% accuracy rate 46.8% of the time. This change in performance is a strong indicator of the impact that data can have on the overall performance of the model. After isolating on the two sources of benchmark data, it is clear that model performance can vary based on those criteria.

10% ACCURACY RATE BY COUNTY – APPRAISAL BENCHMARK ONLY

COUNTY, ST	AVM 1 10% AR	AVM 2 10% AR	AVM 3 10% AR	AVM 4 10% AR
SACRAMENTO, CA	21.95%	27.44%	22.56%	28.05%
COOK, IL	26.14%	21.59%	26.14%	26.14%
ALAMEDA, CA	27.78%	20.83%	23.61%	27.78%
FAIRFAX, VA	25.71%	24.29%	24.29%	25.71%
SAN JOAQUIN, CA	20.37%	27.78%	22.22%	29.63%
ARAPAHOE, CO	22.00%	24.00%	20.00%	34.00%
STANISLAUS, CA	21.28%	25.53%	23.40%	29.79%

JEFFERSON, KY	19.57%	32.61%	15.22%	32.61%
SONOMA, CA	23.26%	23.26%	23.26%	30.23%
ORANGE, FL	26.19%	26.19%	16.67%	30.95%
NASSAU, NY	21.95%	26.83%	21.95%	29.27%
BERGEN, NJ	24.24%	24.24%	24.24%	27.27%
DOUGLAS, CO	24.24%	24.24%	24.24%	27.27%
DENVER, CO	21.88%	18.75%	28.13%	31.25%
WASHINGTON, OR	18.75%	31.25%	18.75%	31.25%
CUYAHOGA, OH	25.81%	19.35%	25.81%	29.03%

It is noteworthy that with the benchmark type segmented into the groups, that the AVM 4 model's performance is much better on appraisal benchmarks compared to contract price. This may be an indication that the comparative models are making some use of MLS, or other data sources which provides some insight into the contract price.

While this analysis has demonstrated that the AVM 4 model appears competitive with three of the commonly used AVMs in the market, none of the AVMs are very accurate.

Imagine purchasing a $10,000,000 RMBS portfolio and using the four models and the best performing properties provided values 46.8% of the time within 10% of the sale price or appraised value. That would mean that 53.2% of the time, the values fell outside of the 10% range. Would that give you comfort knowing that many homeowners are only investing 3% to 10% equity into a home? What would happen if a market started down a road of depreciation due to local or national economic conditions? Or what about a natural disaster like a hurricane or tornado hitting a portion of your inventory. The major employer may have relocated overseas, a recent natural disaster (tornado, hurricane, earthquake, etc.) may keep new buyers out of the market, interest rates increase, or oil falls to $40 per barrel; all these would affect house demand in all or certain markets.

QCLV

The AVM models get infinitely better when quantitative ratings for quality, condition, location and view are assigned to the sales!

Walk through 100 homes and rank them from 1 (best) to 6 (worst) for quality, condition, location and view. Then two days later, take the same 100 homes and rank them again. Would your second ranking match your first ranking? Then two weeks later, how would your third ranking compare? Now, if 100 real estate professionals ranked those 100 homes, would their rankings be the same? The answer, of course, is "highly unlikely."

Appraisers are required to rank homes, they appraise and the comparable sales and listings they use, under this rating system. So will they remember how they previously rated that subject property and comparables? Better yet, how do they know how other appraisers and professionals rated those comparables?

Without processing big data, it is highly unlikely that any industry can have the transparency needed to see what was done in your analysis, much less all of your peers.

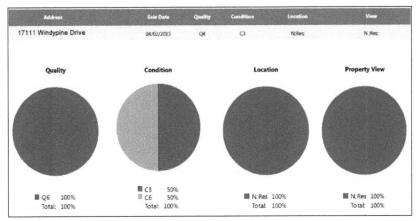

Adding QCLV enhances the accuracy of AVMs and the VRA conclusions to as high as 90%+. This is a substantial improvement over the previous conclusions and is at an accuracy level that would allow buyers of RMBS and others to more accurately price the inventory. With millions of homes selling annually, this would take a large team of researchers or a combination of desk reviewers with field inspectors, like appraisers, to rate every home sale in the U.S. Besides FNMA, Enriched Data is the only other company we know of analyzing, rating, and collecting the data.

This discussion should have opened up your thoughts to the potential of big data and ways it can be filtered to help you differentiate yourself in the market to be more successful. Knowledge about your targeted investment, monitoring not only your asset, but all assets like it will allow you to excel and move into a portfolio ownership platform.

THE NEWCOMERS

This discussion will showcase the best of the best. Those who took a little and made a lot, and those who got a lot and made more.

At 8 years old, Albert Fürst von Thurn und Taxis was found on Forbes' billionaire list. When he turned 18 he officially inherited a billion dollar fortune. Then he went on to complete college and enhanced his fortune. By the time he was 30 his fortune was worth about $3.8 billion! He is also a bachelor and races cars; the epitome of the free and easy lifestyles. How does the 12th prince in a long line of distinguished Germans enhance his incredible wealth? His patriarchal family structure helped Albert manage his ownership of 36,000 hectares of woodland real estate, income-producing real estate and art.

Perenna Kei at age 24 had a net worth of $1.3 billion, holding the title of the world's youngest billionaire. As Logan Property Holdings' chairman and CEO, Kei did not take her responsibility to hold onto the family's wealth lightly. She holds a bachelor's degree in economics and finance from the University of London.

Yang Huiyan at age 32 had a net worth of $6.9 billion. China's richest woman. As Vice Chairman of real estate developer Country Garden, she helped position the company for its initial public offering in 2007. Then she was recognized on Forbes' list of China's richest with a net worth of $16 billion.

Ayman Hariri at age 35 had a net worth of $1.2 billion. As head of Saudi Oger, one of Saudi Arabia's biggest construction companies, her company won a $653 million contract in January 2013 to build a local branch of the Jean Nouvel-designed Louvre museum in Abu Dhabi.

Ayman's younger brother, Fahd Hariri at age 33 also had a net worth of $1.2 billion. Graduating from the Ecole Spéciale d'Architecture de Paris in 2004, he went on to develop residential buildings.

Lawrence Ho at age 37 had a net worth of $3 billion. Mr. Ho and his father Stanley Ho own Melco Crown Entertainment, with casinos in Macau and Manila.

Worldwide, 20 and 30-year-olds are inheriting massive amounts of wealth. These are just a few examples of individuals who strived for educational excellence in order to responsibly manage the family's fortunes. The transfer of real estate wealth is about to accelerate to levels the world has never seen before.

So what can you do? If you have real estate holdings, even if it is just the home you live in, will your heirs responsibly manage those assets when you leave this world? How do you empower your heirs to expand the real estate holdings you have acquired?

Let us explore one of the unique real estate purchases that the wealthy and famous indulge in; purchasing an island. While it sounds incredibly exciting, owning an island is not as much fun as most would envision. My colleagues have pegged it as the "3 to 5-Year Island Itch." Once the island is purchased, significant capital has to go into building boat and plane access. Then you have to build the infrastructure, like, water, sewer and electricity plus the structures to house it all. And you just can't call for a repairman, order pizza for delivery or have your nails done by a professional. Who do you find to take care of your island when you are gone? So many who purchase an island find the "money pit" is a never-ending experience.

And for most island owners, the lack of friends close by is worse than the "money pit" of having to build your own electrical generating facility, marina, roads, dock or even runway, after you buy the island. You have to bring your friends along or create your own imaginary relationships; remember Tom Hank's best-friend-forever (BFF) "Wilson." Or maybe you can find an island where the neighboring islands are owned by cool people.

THE RICH & FAMOUS ISLAND OWNERS
OF THE EXUMA CAYS

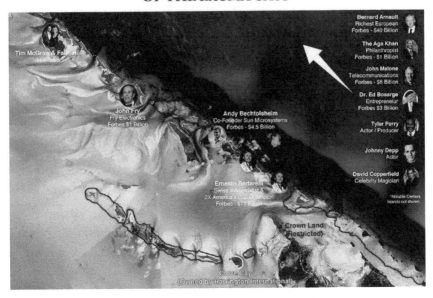

It would be quite a task to have all these owners visit their islands at the same time! Then you would have to determine whose island you have dinner at. A hurricane could certainly put a damper on the party!

After years of planning and infrastructure completion, a new upscale resort with golf course was under construction for a $300,000,000 resort that was being built on the island of Anguilla, in the Caribbean. It attracted the Martha Vineyard's millionaires and billionaires. Homes were priced over $10,000,000 each. After inspecting the property multiple times over the years, decided to send the young apprentice for a quick inspection to view the progress of the development for an appraisal. However, the call from him upon landing on the island was a shrill of wind and disruptive panic, "a hurricane is coming and they are evacuating the island!" As he was still on the airport tarmac following the 12-minute flight from Saint-Martin, it was impressed on him that if he did not get some pictures of the updated construction, we would lose weeks and affect the loan closing. Multiple calls during the 15 minute drive in a cab to the property further enforced the wind and panic noises and luckily followed with a successful inspection, albeit pictures of flying trees and small animals. So plan your inspections accordingly!

An island ownership can also get messy during a divorce settlement; do you split the island in half? One could take the runway and the other the dock for access. Then one of the spouses could be scornful enough to build a fence down the middle of the island in order to not see their cheating ex.

Now comes the millennials, age 18 to 35. With technology advances doubling about every seven years, millennials are spending all of their disposable income on gadgets they can wear on their wrist or slimmed-down hand-held devices that track everything from spending habits and health of the owner to social media interaction.

Did the baby boomer's $19 trillion-dollar increase of the U.S. deficit screw them for eternity? How does this generation follow in the footsteps of the millionaire tech geeks that made fortunes before them?

When Twitter went public, it created about 1,600 multi-millionaires in a single day. Over the next three months, the average upper-end house price in San Francisco and Silicon Valley escalated over 30%. That 28-year-old new multi-millionaire bought everything from new X-Box games to sports cars and expensive homes! The millennials need for "instant gratification" and in an age of "everyone gets a trophy just for playing" is changing the way millennials invest not only in their future, but in the future foundation of raising money for real estate. From 2017 to 2020, we will see evolutionary ideas on how to invest and the ability for everyone, not just millionaires, to invest in real estate.

Whatever age, regardless of what someone starts with, implementing a plan to grow is a key to those who succeed. Knowledge not only at the micro level, but also across the property type at differing locations will allow insight into trends that may soon allow you to provide predictive analytics.

LEVERAGING INTERNATIONAL EXPERTISE

If you have ever watched "Shark Tank," you may not have noticed that in many product investment offerings one of the prospective investors will ask "have you explored product production overseas?" If recommended for many manufactured products, then why should real estate research and analysis support be solely U.S. based? In 2016, most of the billion dollar companies who research, sort, aggregate and delivery real estate information have embraced and international culture of working across international boundaries.

While the "number of clicks" a website gets can drive millions of dollars in marketing revenue, most applications rely on the "click fee" for revenue. Thousands of websites offer real estate offerings, services, and enhancements in marketing. Most of the industry leaders use a combination of cloud applications, algorithms, sophisticated websites, and intense data research. The latter, intense data research, is difficult with U.S. labor costs.

So what is intense data research? Imagine that you have friend who is the pool business. He asks you to find every home sale in your city, within a few weeks of acquisition, over $200,000, and does not have a swimming pool. What a great marketing strategy, to notify home buyers that a new pool could come with their new purchase!

While the job of tracking every home purchase that does not have a pool in a large city is massive, the pool company would still have to have a marketing machine to reach every homeowner. That could amount 30,000+ homeowners in a year. Again, another significant task to consider.

Offshore labor could be employed to track the home sales through a subscription service, although it would not be cost effective in the U.S. Those sales could be cross-checked with county records for ownership information, and further researched for homeowner contact data, social media, and phone contact lists would provide the Business to People (B2P) leads. Then, the data would be uploaded into a Client Relationship Management (CRM) program to send emails, periodic updates, etc. With the typical home selling every 6 to 10 years, it would not take long for most homeowners in the city to be very familiar with the pool company.

Jones Lang LaSalle (JLL) suggests facilities management is one of the top three expense line items for owners of income producing properties. Bryan Jacobs, Managing Director, Solutions Development, states, "...strategic sourcing professionals to create value and reduce costs through worker enablement - especially when coupled with thoughtful IT and HR strategies." The integration of internet applications into an offshore enterprise helps the quality control and time management issues that come from remote employment. Chat boards are preferred over email interaction. Project management boards are also needed to see progress. And seeing in real time the business platform applications, e.g., accounting, management, computer programming or data processing, is key to progress. In today's world, time is not on your side, and a 10-hour time difference between operations can cost much more that the labor savings if business objectives are not being completed.

John Santora, President, Chief Executive Officer, Corporate Occupier & Investor Services (CIS), Cushman & Wakefield, Inc. reported in their 2013 publication, found:

- Occupiers are struggling with cost, expansion, and process alignment;

- Occupiers have yet to settle on a preferred outsource model;

- Investors are facing tighter regulations for owning and operating property;

- Investors are increasingly seeking asset management services; and

- Service providers are assuming more risk on behalf of their clients.

Their survey of 300 corporate clients asked respondents to rank in order of importance the critical factors that are influencing their decision to outsource real estate services:

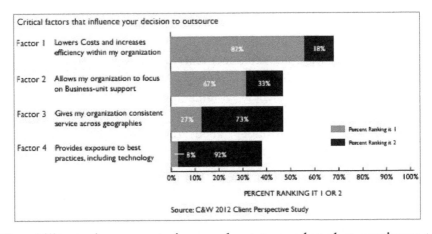

Critical factors that influence your decision to outsource

Factor 1	Lowers Costs and increases efficiency within my organization	82% 18%
Factor 2	Allows my organization to focus on Business-unit support	67% 33%
Factor 3	Gives my organization consistent service across geographies	27% 73%
Factor 4	Provides exposure to best practices, including technology	8% 92%

Percent Ranking it 1
Percent Ranking it 2

PERCENT RANKING IT 1 OR 2

Source: C&W 2012 Client Perspective Study

The ability to lower costs in a real estate market that continues to increase its level of transparency is the most cited influence to outsource business solutions oversees. The fact that real estate investors can now view real estate offerings throughout the country has tended to equalize pricing and omit the occurrences of high capitalization rates where pricing anomalies can occur. A high capitalization rate equates to a lower price (net operating income divided by capitalization rate = price). If investors can view all real estate offerings equally, then those outliers can be seen easily and low priced assets should be the selected investment targets.

Business Example

About eight years ago, Patrick O'Connor started Pathfinder Analytics (http://www.pathfinderanalysis.com/) which today has a personnel base of over 500. Patrick O'Connor & Associates (OCA) has the largest real estate research team of any major real estate firm to directly source, survey and update U.S. real estate data. And it is the lowest cost operation of any competitive database firm. Pathfinder Business Analysis, LTD (PFBA) is registered in Tamil Nadu, India and millions are spent annually to perform programming, data entry, indexing, research, judgment research, and customer service. Virtually all employees are college graduates and 10% have advanced degrees. The professionals are highly skilled in real estate research and generate unique options to access data.

U.S. property records and the people who interact with that real estate are included in the data base. Networks of mortgage bankers, appraisers, investors, owners, buyers, real estate brokers, and business to real estate service companies throughout the U.S. use the data daily. Through cloud applications, and other methods of achieving retrieval of the data, enhancements from those professionals enrich the data to increase the accuracy. Larger users take API or data uploads into their client management systems to enhance their databases to achieve growth business goals. Technology applications developed by Pathfinder feed data to professionals in web applications like www.enricheddata.com.

Speak more than one language? If so, there is a good chance that there are companies needing your service on a contractual basis. Conversely, there is even a better chance that there are contract workers in other countries that speak that language have an education and specialty willing to do contract work for you and your clients at a fraction of the cost of what you can do it for yourself.

International careers are providing opportunities for college graduates to pre-retirees. Providing expertise and support to an international team allows many cross-cultural individuals to become cohesive team members and thrive in markets where competition is bringing down fees. Not having a vast real estate knowledge base does not prevent you from working in the real estate business. Companies providing applications and data that real estate professionals use need your help!

WORK FROM HOME LEVERAGING BIG DATA TO MAKE BIG MONEY

There are tens of thousands of real estate professionals working from home. But they need the same tools and knowledge base as a professional in a large real estate company. Let's discuss ways each of these parties can perform on a level playing field.

The ability to search property sales and rents that most search engines provide is enhanced by the ability to search mortgages (borrower, lender, termination date of loan, etc.), market reports, find selected tenants, etc.

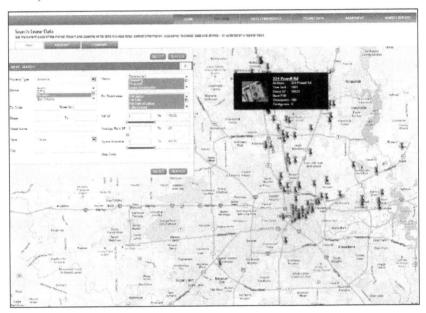

The information about ownership is as important as information on real estate. Different homeowners take care of their homes differently. An empty-nester's home's interior would be significantly different than that of a family with five children. Class A high-rise tenants have finishes substantially different than Class C space in small low-rise buildings. We can collect a lot of information about a Fortune 100 company, but not so much on a local company owned by a husband and wife team.

If interested in the commercial real estate space, you will need to know about tenants and how they are categorized using standardized classification systems.

Businesses in the USA are classified by a Standard Industrial Classification (SIC) and North American Industry Classification System (NAICS) code. SIC is a system for classifying industries by a four-digit code. Established in the United States in 1937, it is used by government agencies to classify industry areas. NAICS is the Federal statistical agencies' standard in classifying businesses for the purpose of collecting, analyzing, and publishing statistical data related to the U.S. business economy. NAICS was developed under the direction of the Office of Management and Budget (OMB), and adopted in 1997. By using these two classifications in a database, tenant-leased spaces and owner occupied properties can be monitored, searched, and evaluated.

For example, fast food restaurants are categorized under SIC Code 5812 and NAICS Code 722513. The first two digits of the four digit SIC code fall into the following business categories:

SIC CODES	BUSINESS CATEGORY
01-09	Agriculture, Forestry, Fishing
10-14	Mining
15-17	Construction
20-39	Manufacturing
40-49	Transportation & Public Utilities
50-51	Wholesale Trade
52-59	Retail Trade
60-67	Finance, Insurance, Real Estate
70-89	Services
91-99	Public Administration

The businesses can be further defined within each major category, a sample of which is shown:

SIC CODES	DETAILED BUSINESS CATEGORY
52-59	Retail Trade
52	Building Materials, Hardware, Garden Supply, and Mobile Home Dealers

53	General Merchandise Stores
54	Food Stores
55	Automotive Dealers and Gasoline Service Stations

Then by adding a third digit, more detail business categories emerge:

SIC CODES	MORE DETAILED BUSINESS CATEGORY
54	Food Stores
541	Grocery Stores
542	Meat and Fish (Seafood) Markets, including Freezer Provisioners
543	Fruit Stores and Vegetable Markets
544	Candy, Nut, and Confectionery Stores

Finally, the last of the four digits provides the most detailed business category:

5421	Meat and Fish (Seafood) Markets, including Freezer Provisioners

And within SIC Code 5421, retailers like Omaha Steaks and Armour-Eckrich Meats are categorized. The ability to define a target tenant opens service and product providers the ability to pinpoint desired tenant types. Additionally, overlaying physical footprints on those businesses, allows spatial requirements to be researched. For example, a high rise office has a title company vacate a 3,000 square foot first floor suite. Since there is no retail in the building, management and leasing recognize the need for a deli restaurant to enhance their tenant profile. The ability to search all deli restaurants in the market and reach out to those tenants to see if they would expand into the vacant space is now easier than ever. You can even do it from your phone.

The codes for NAICS are a little more detailed, as shown by the sample base business category types:

Code	Industry Title
11	Agriculture, Forestry, Fishing and Hunting
21	Mining
22	Utilities

23	Construction
31-33	Manufacturing
42	Wholesale Trade
44-45	Retail Trade
48-49	Transportation and Warehousing

Then the categories evolve into the following:

Codes	Titles
44-45	Retail Trade
441110	New Car Dealers
441120	Used Car Dealers
441210	Recreational Vehicle Dealers
441222	Boat Dealers
441228	Motorcycle, ATV, and All Other Motor Vehicle Dealers
441310	Automotive Parts and Accessories Stores
441320	Tire Dealers
442110	Furniture Stores
442210	Floor Covering Stores
442291	Window Treatment Stores
442299	All Other Home Furnishings Stores
443141	Household Appliance Stores
443142	Electronics Stores
444110	Home Centers

A new pet grooming business can search for 453910 - Pet and Pet Supplies Stores and locate where local homeowners purchase upscale dog food products.

When looking for businesses, recently purchased properties, and sellers for recently sold properties, professionals want information, not only, on the physical and economic characteristics, but also, detailed contact data on who sold, owns, manages, leases, and lent on these properties. Databases house the information across multiple data providers, but not in a cohesive manner where any data point on real estate and those who interact with that real estate can be searched and filtered. Aggregating the following would provide an interesting database to see base information on real estate ownership and those who help transact that information.

- Real estate professionals;

- Deeds – A deed is proof of a transaction occurred – sale or lien of some type; and

- Deeds of trust are a recorded mortgage loan instrument.

By putting these deeds and deeds of trust into a standardized, manageable, and searchable database with rent, sales, and tenant data, the combined contact lists provide a "Network of Real Estate Professionals" contacts that can be managed for marketing and distribution lists:

- Vendors providing real estate services (insurance, pest control, security, cleaning, renovation, management, leasing, electric/utility, cable/TV, etc.) require the data and contacts for existing and new businesses;

- Businesses who market directly to consumers (grocers, auto sales, restaurants, vacation venues, etc.); and

- Brokers, lenders, mortgage bankers – parties who want contact with owners, managers, brokers, etc.

Be Strategic

Finding a solution to a business or real estate problem is the best way to start a new business. Then combine that solution with what you do well and it will become your passion. Apply your skills to the solution and "build your community." Invite family, friends and their associates to be part of your domain. Build a network that can "scale." Social media is a great way to get the word out. Attend conferences, conventions, and community events. It takes work, but connecting to your community builds your brand. If you are not the social media type, then bring someone on your team that loves to shine in crowds.

And your brand needs to be digital, because the smart phone connection is the way to stay in touch with your community. Having a smart phone application that people can connect with you is better than any business card.

Jack Nicklaus is one of the most recognized name brand in U.S. Jack Nicklaus' company, over a decade ago, developed a proprietary program that could layout an 18-hole golf course in a few hours, but only if a detailed topographical map, surveys of the property and even the trees were mapped. Numerous hours were spent tweaking the design. Once the layout was completed, a "fly" over could be computerized, allowing Jack to view the tees, greens and fairways depending on the time of the year. Even the path of the sun could be tracked, to allow a view of how the sunlight hit the grass. Trees would be kept or removed based on these factors, to allow premium grass growth. Thousands of golfers pay premium green fees to play these spectacular golf courses all over the world.

Fashion-conscious men and women wear Nicklaus-brand quality clothing daily to work, play, and golf outings. However, golf was on the decline in the first half of the 2010 decade. A Nicklaus-branded golf development was not built in the U.S. for four and one-half years prior to 2016. So how do you market a to-be-built Nicklaus-brand golf development in Lexington, Kentucky?

Well, if you had the address, phone number, email, and LinkedIn address of every homeowner in the U.S. who lives within the same zip code as a Nicklaus-brand golf course, you would have a good start, wouldn't you? Then add equestrian to the data search, and you open up a larger market segment of Kentuckians and others who also love the outdoors.

As a real estate agent in Lexington, you would want to grab every golfer with a low handicap (typically 14 or below indicates an excellent golfer) by researching the Professional Golf Association database and direct them to the Legacy Point Project.

Every heard of "First to Market?" Businesses that offer "First to Market" products tend not only to be successful, but also can scale quickly to significant revenue. As others start to enter this space, "First to Market" or "First Mover Advantage," businesses tend to retain high percentages of clients, even if their product is inferior to the competitive products.

Knowledge of a market, even as small as the home value trends in a zip code, can unleash tremendous wealth.

Home equity loan programs are difficult to sell in markets with stable values. But when markets appreciate, this program unleashes billions and even trillions of dollars of capital to homeowners who can revitalize an economy. New porches, pool additions, tile and carpet replacements, and even vacations of a lifetime are now available to homeowners who just retain homeownership long enough to realize the incredible wealth builder that market appreciation to their primary residence brings.

And the pool builder, home remodeler and roofer should all capitalize on marketing in these locations. As all cities do not appreciate equally, neither do all homes in a particular zip code or neighborhood within larger markets. And anyone can access home price trends in markets and particular segments in a market on the internet - just search "home price trends and name your city or zip or neighborhood" and you'll see over 10 pages of data providers providing snippets of information that can help you see what is going on in your real estate market.

Be mobile! I'm not just referring to your phone, but your business. Mobile businesses that can move to markets where significant changes have occurred typically have "First Mover Advantage." A renovation company in Houston, Texas, may have a good business tackling the occasional storm and decade lag in hurricane damage, but if that company can mobilize to every, tornado, flood, storm, and hurricane-damaged area in the country, then their revenue can grow exponentially. Like food trucks that move the restaurant experience to where the people are, businesses that can adapt to these business trends may be able to capture that "First Mover Advantage."

Now let's talk about real estate investment. Baby boomers playing in the real estate investment game reached out to their friends, associates, and colleagues to take them to lunch, have board meetings and fly around the county for "sit down meetings." Phone banks that practiced cold calling irritate homeowners with only a fraction of success in reaching someone who would listen to the sales pitch.

Mass mailings of 3"x5" flyers show up on Wednesdays in mailboxes throughout the country and most homeowners dispose of the flyers in the recycle bin (if they have that option available). Timeshare and fractional resort developers entice prospects with a "free vacation" if they will sit down in a room for 2+ hours with over-zealous sales teams trying to entice them to "buy."

Traditional investment in real estate had the well-healed Trumps of the world courting wealthy real estate investors through Real Estate Investment Trusts, Limited Liability Companies, and Syndications. Most investors were required to pony up at least $50,000 to $1,000,000 on a single investment that offered little transparency on the asset classes economic positioning in the competitive market in which it was situated. Some investments were spread across multiple real estate asset classes (office, retail, apartments and industrial), with even less clarity on the multiple assets' ability to appreciate. And most of the time the big winner was the developer or hedge fund manager, as a result of the various fees collected during the holding of the assets.

Today's millennials connect through social media with hundreds and, for some, thousands of people they have never met. A great idea can go viral in hours and reach millions of people. And Facebook allows everyone to have their own website. These websites allow every domestic engineer (we used to call them housewives) to have their individual wants, needs, ideas and brand showcased across the World Wide Web, sometimes better than most businesses. These websites allow individuals to bring not only their friends together, but also their community and beyond. Now add social media to the equation, plus texts, phone calls, tweets and pings which are sent ~~go~~ out in the hundreds of millions every day. Now, add your photo to all of your social media publications and emails. Change up the photo, showcasing your abilities, hobbies and interests. Dog lover include your buddy in the photo!

Today, every person can have a web-based presence that showcases amazing projects and ideas to interested patrons and contributors for a few dollars per month. Groundbreaking ideas can become reality in minutes. Real estate investors can be brought together like never before due to relaxed regulatory requirements for courting "Accredited Investors." Crowdfunding is the resurgence of multiple parties coming together to make a single investment, but at meteoric levels.

The Securities Act of 1933 has kept investors and developers from soliciting small investors. However, in 2013, the JOBS Act permitted crowdfunding. Platforms slowly sprang up across the country, emerging with "pools" of investors putting up as little as $5,000 and even using self-directed 401K money, to invest in typical real estate investment vehicles, such as, rental homes, apartments and multi-tenant retail, and office space. Credited investors of all sizes can access thousands of sponsors' investments in need of funding.

Massolution reported investors funded $1 billion in crowdfunding in 2014 and climbed to $2.5 billion by the end of 2015. We are anticipating exponential increases thereafter, as technology takes center stage with electronic documents, E-Signature, and as social media increases the number of investors savvy enough to make a deal. Now, the trend is expanding internationally.

Funding real estate deals through crowdfunding allows investors to diversify their portfolios at lower investment levels than previously available. The following reflect some of the leading crowdfunding companies:

1. RealtyWealth;

2. Hotel Innvestor;

3. CoAssets;

4. GroundBreaker;

5. Patch of Land;

6. Prodigy Network;

7. iFunding;

8. CrowdRealty;

9. CrowdVested; and

10. Realty Mogul.

It will be interesting to see how many of these companies are around in 10 years. There are a few different types of crowdfunding:

1. Debt;

2. NNN (typically single-tenant real estate leased by a tenant who pays all fixed, operation, and capital expenditure expenses); and

3. Equity.

To put it into perspective, the stock market is the true definition of crowdfunding. Investors can put their money into any registered company anywhere in the world; companies that sell drinks, medicinal cures, or rock and roll.

Debt crowdfunding typically reflects a loan on a project where the security is the lien and the loan amount is typically less than the market value of the asset, say 75%. The sponsors pay the investors a high portion of the annual loan amount, typically from 7% to 12%. Amortizing loans also have a portion of the principle paid back with each payment. At the termination of the loan, the investors are paid the remaining principle back.

Triple Net (NNN) investments act very similar to debt investing. Single tenants like Walgreens, McDonalds, and other retailers occupy buildings and pay rent under lease terms generally from 10 to 20 years. Because the tenants pay fixed (taxes and insurance) and operating (utilities, repairs, etc.) expenses in addition to rent, investors are provided a fairly "no-load" revenue stream. Typically there are periodic rent increases, the ability for depreciation deductions and potential property appreciation to enhance the periodic returns and the property's residual sale price at the termination of the lease.

Crowdfunding for equity allows cash-strapped sponsors to raise capital for all types of projects. Investments can be purchased with 100% cash, or an equity portion of the investment can be leveraged with debt.

Now, more than ever, investors need the tools that the experts use when evaluating real estate assets.

Entrepreneurial Economy

The ability to be your own boss is the new economy. The days of working for a company for 25 years and retiring with a "huuuuge" retirement package are over. Even working as an Uber driver gives individuals the power to work, after hours, for themselves. Ideas of careers have changed from what even our fathers and mothers were thinking and now their families and loved ones are embracing this change and individualism. Their success depends on what their commitment is, but that commitment can now take the shape of talent rather than time.

A .Net programmer can take on a contract job, engaged over the internet by a company on the other side of the world, without ever meeting someone from the company. Individuals can compete to deliver a schematic of a new website and based on the preliminary deliverable, that person gets the $2,000 contract. And today, that person can also be a chef, massage therapist or even a pizza delivery driver.

By 2020, it is estimated that half the U.S. workforce will have an entrepreneurial gig. Knowing how to use technology tools that process big data will be a key to those who succeed. Predictive analytics will allow someone, who sees a problem, to provide a solution. Those providing the best solutions have the ability to scale the business not only nationally, but internationally. The internet allows anyone to build, market, sell, and grow.

Smartphones allow products to be marketed real-time, at point-of-contact and at both a "shot-gun" (across a broad market) and "rifle" (to a specific prospect type) marketing approach. Having your own app, website and/or internet marketed product can provide a financial freedom our grandparents never thought of. The ability to order organic vegetables from around the world benefits our lifestyle and the economics of third world countries. Certain people are more efficient during certain times of the day and knowing how to write computer code to deliver digital products that make professionals in an industry more efficient allows them to work part-time at the hours they choose.

Regardless of age, education or background, the ability to work as an entrepreneur at the hours you choose has never been easier. About half of Americans realize that to get ahead and be independent, they will need to participate as an entrepreneur. The other half will likely not fulfill their economic potential. The primary reasons to create an internet company are:

1. Supplement income of current job;

2. Work when you want;

3. Fulfill your brand identity; and

4. Create financial independence.

Speed to market is key, because if you do not try to solve a problem, then someone else will. Working from home and interacting with remote business associates who work not only from their cities, but from cities around the world, provide business networks that solve problems quickly. While any age group can work in this new economy, retirees can drive their new businesses as well as millennials.

Health and wellness is important in this new economy, so working from home does not mean fast food and lethargic lifestyles. Decades of missing Little League baseball games and dance recitals will be in the past. While we may never get rid of adrenalin drinks to "shock" our bodies into action, an internet business can provide its own level of testosterone.

The great thing about an internet business is that once you get someone's credit card and a monthly payment, you tend to keep them engaged longer than a typical retail store. However, selling directly to consumers, or even businesses, takes a catchy marketing and sales platform to attract leads. Then those leads need some "beta" testing to determine if they really want to be a client. At the point of sale, those clients need to know that your business is going to protect their personal data, especially credit card information. The days of taking credit card numbers over the phone and paper contracts are over; the liability associated with stolen credit card numbers is well-known by the largest bankers and retailers in the world.

There are a number of business platforms that allow independent contractors to join a team of like-kind professionals to perform the most complicated business solutions. These positions can accommodate night and weekend work. These temporary work positions can lead to full-time positions for those who excel. Temporary to permanent solutions are not only good for employers, but allow employees to see if they fit into the business platform and the social network of the company.

Freelance contractor postings for new web pages, programming projects and data filtering applications bring results from all over the world. In many instances, there are more international respondents to programming and data processing than respondents from the U.S. That is because countries around the world have found that IT and programming education provides employment opportunities outside of their current community, without having the resident relocate. By 2050, executives are of the opinion that freelance entrepreneurs will make up over 75% of technology jobs. Companies put out on the internet a scope of work and freelance/entrepreneurs will showcase their "white pages" interpretation of the solution by providing "wireframe" deliverables, sketches, graphs, flow charts and other examples on how they interpreted the solution to the scope of work requested. The company looking for the solution then selects the best tech provider and engages in a multi-step completion of the assignment. In many situations, freelancers can earn more money part-time than they can in their full-time jobs. The security of having a day job, coupled with the upside potential of increased hourly billing rates at times that are convenient to the techie, creates a growing economy.

Tech providers can bid on only those assignments that meet their unique abilities, while providing workloads and times that maximize their social schedules. The ability to control, and even dictate their schedules are much more favorable than any full-time job. Literally within minutes, creative professionals can create new contract opportunities. So rather than interviewing for full-time jobs, they can bid on new assignments daily, weekly and monthly at per hour levels exponentially above what they can get paid through full-time work at multi-national corporations. If you have the ability to put your business solutions in an app (works on a smart phone), then you and your company could be on the path to being part of an elite group of Unicorns (private, upstart companies that are valued at over $1 billion). Entrepreneurship now is a focus of individuals looking to create their future employment path. They can take control of their future with the goal of positively affecting their lifestyle.

Be an entrepreneur, even if a couple hours a week. Your family and friends will appreciate your efforts and tenacity. Even if you do not make a fortune, if you are doing something you love, then rewards will follow.

THE PLAYERS

This discussion will review who the industry experts are and what do they do:

1. Developers
2. Investors
3. Brokers
4. Appraisers
5. Lenders
6. Major Big Data Players

Developers

Developers make it happen. They are at the forefront of the industry that builds projects from the "ground up" or rehabs existing projects into modern buildings. With this group comes the greatest financial risk. Insufficient funds to complete construction, environmental and local community lawsuits from those favoring "no-growth," government permitting and oversight, and a lack of demand for the product upon completion due to increased competition or changing economics during the construction cycle are just some examples of the risks developers are faced with.

One of the largest office projects ever developed in Latin America took three years to construct. At the start of construction, rents were $50 per square foot, but fell to less than $30 per square foot by the time of completion, making the project not economically feasible. One California developer had been sued consecutively over 17 years, blocking development of what would be a spectacular resort hotel and condominium project. Even projects that take less than a year to construct can experience influences that diminish the economic viability during the construction process.

With higher risk comes higher returns and successful developers yield their investors the highest returns in the industry.

Investors

Investors are the life-blood of the commercial real estate market. They trade assets through various real estate life-cycles, some using contrarian mentality by buying when the market is depreciating, others buying for stable yields when the market is appreciating. A simple search of "investors" yields 397 million search results. News agencies provide specialized real estate sections for investors to review transactions and see what analysts are suggesting is the hot market or property type. Also, news agencies report on institutional companies advertising to attract investors to their management platform and networks and reaching out to connect investors to their assets. Of course, they like to see who is lending on, selling and buying the big deals. Just recently, crowdfunding and other groups have emerged to enter the investment domain, but most focus on smaller assets. "We buy houses" have sprung up across the internet and can even be found on paper signs on medians at local intersections.

So how do investors become successful? It is all about yield: returns from buying assets at a discount or many, like REITs and foreign investors willing to pay market price, to achieve a secure return on and of the investment. While most focus on the upside, the most important topics investors must deal with is the potential for downside risk and the illiquidity of having to sell real estate in a potentially declining market.

Brokers

Brokers are the transaction specialists. From residential brokers who drive neighborhoods daily, to seasoned commercial appraisers who assist buyers and sellers of the largest instructional real estate assets in the world, brokers provide a medium for open market exchanges. The goal in contracting with a broker is to get a lower price or rent than one could normally get if negotiating alone. An owner would engage a seller's broker in order to achieve a higher price. In any case, the buyer's, tenant's or seller's broker would need to convince their client their cost for service will be offset by the savings or increased price.

Brokers are typically incentive-based, taking a percentage of the price or rental amount as a fee. But the market is competitive. While residential brokers strive for 6.0% fees, with the ability to split the fee 50%/50% with a buyer's broker, commercial broker fees can fall to 1.0% or less on multi-million dollar sales. In the 1980's, few commercial brokerage fees topped $1,000,000; now it is commonplace when transacting large real estate assets, $10,000,000+ fees can be obtained.

State licensing with the requirement for continuing education keeps this group engaged and informed. Two professional tiers are typical; brokers who are seasoned professionals, sometimes enveloped around a business, which mentor the second tier salespeople with typically less time in the business or less educational background.

Appraisers

The appraisal industry was essentially established under regulatory pressure to provide "referees" between lenders and borrowers. Over 1,000 data points are typically inputted into one of four industry report writers that help the residential lending business remain compliant and provide uniform appraisal report deliverables. Lenders who are federally regulated are required to engage an appraiser as part of the loan closing process. A picture of how this industry operates follows:

- Two-thirds of industry professionals will be retiring by 2025.

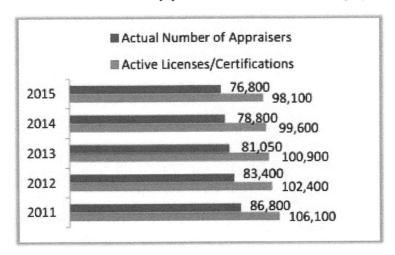

- Changes in the appraisal industry have come from "big brother" Fannie Mae implementing collateral underwriter, aging of appraisers with few millennials entering the industry, and lenders only getting appraisals for less than 25% of loans and loan renewals. All this has contributed to an industry in decline for both professionals and their income. There are a declining number of appraisers each year and there is little incentive to: 1) train new appraisers or 2) encourage young people to become appraisers.

- The method for preparing appraisals has changed significantly in the last 40 years, from Selectric typewriters and carbon paper, moving to Commodore computers and floppy disks and two decades ago, Multimate, Word Perfect, and 1-2-3 for commercial. Now we have Word and Excel to prepare commercial appraisal reports and personal computer-based software for residential appraisals.

The supplemental programs to do analysis (cash flow applications, on-line cost segregation models) are expensive and have not gained traction in the market. Further, they do not increase efficiency for the appraisers. Residential appraisers are not encouraging their children to enter the business due to the level of earnings. The U.S. Government has enacted laws and requirements which have caused Appraisal Management Companies (AMCs) increased fragmentation in the appraisal industry making it more difficult for appraisers to invest in technology. These factors have brought the average-size appraisal firm to less than two people per company.

Future trends that will reshape how appraisers do business will include:

1. On-line software that reduces the time to write an appraisal report by 30% to 50%.

2. Software linked to subject property, rental, and comparable sale databases.

3. Analytics included with the software; helping the appraisers to support adjustments.

4. The average age of an appraiser is 62 years old, and they have not been training millennials at any level to replace them as they retire. While the benefits for training appraisers include: 1) increased revenue, 2) young trainees can help move along the technology learning curve, and 3) building an exit strategy for retirement, restrictive regulatory requirements are a disincentive to the industry's legacy professionals to train replacements.

5. Lenders are getting more access to big data and use it in analytics to evaluate the credibility of an appraisal. These

lenders are using those large databases and analytics to increase transparency in the appraisal process.

6. Report writers will respond to the algorithms used by GSEs such as Fannie Mae's collateral underwriter.

7. Fewer appraisers will be generating the same number of appraisals.

8. Commercial data will be supplemented with qualitative fields of data such as quality, condition, location, and view; even psychographics.

9. Additional fields of data will be added to commercial databases to help evaluate land values such as frontage feet, street name, traffic count, and type of street (primary, secondary and tertiary).

10. More consistent data will help appraisers to select the best comparable sales and make the valuation process more transparent for lenders.

11. Crowdsourcing of sections of commercial appraisals (city data, apartment overview for subject city, etc.) will increase efficiency.

12. MLS will become a less important tool. Sites such as Zillow, Trulia, For Sale By Owner, RedFin and the other "Non-MLS listings" will become more prevalent.

13. Appraisers will have exposure if they do not consider all sales, and not just the ones on MLS.

14. Appraiser-oriented data is necessary to efficiently prepare residential appraisals. It simply will not be cost efficient to review 4 or 5 sources of data for comparable sales.

15. Additional fields of data such as QCLV will help the appraiser to: 1) efficiently and effectively select comparable sales; 2) make them aware if their evaluation of a comparable is different than their peers or previous appraisals; and 3) avoid running afoul of collateral underwriter.

16. Millenniums will be the catalyst to effect change in the traditional brokerage model.

17.   The outlook for single-family appraisals in homogeneous neighborhoods is unclear. However, their demise has been predicted for 10+ years.

18.   Appraisers effectively using technology will substantially increase their earnings. Appraisers employing trainees will generate an exit strategy by selling the practice to one of the employees.

Lenders

Lenders have many faces, but one thing is certain, they want your real estate and possibility your entire wealth as collateral for a loan. They have been around since money was invented. They expect the loan to be repaid, with interest and/or fees. Lenders can be banks, mortgage banks, or other financial institutions that lend their own money.

Periods of predatory lending, when lenders take advantage of borrowers, have brought about laws and practice requirements on usury (establish caps on interest rate charges), monitoring residential mortgage bankers and brokers on their business practices and other practices managed through the Office of Comptroller of Currency (OCC).

As a result of inappropriate lending activities in the mid 2000 decade, some of the largest U.S. lenders have paid billions in fines. New laws then cropped up to help mitigate similar motivations for the future. Those new laws are costing companies millions to implement and making them re-evaluate whether they want to be in the home-lending business.

Mortgage brokers help borrowers shop various lenders for the best loan deals. While most borrowers cannot go direct to a life insurance company for a loan, designated mortgage brokers for those companies can. That is important on the commercial lending side, as sophisticated loan processing systems have not been developed on the commercial loan side. However, tools like Rocket Mortgage, Lending Tree, etc. to obtain the best rates on the residential mortgage side have been developed and streamline not only the application process, but the entire loan process all the way to the title company at closing.

For almost 90 years, correspondent lenders have been originating and selling loans. They have the ability to buy other mortgage lender's production and resell it, typically for a higher price. This demand occurred as some lenders burned through their loan portfolio and needed replacement loans to service with their current level of operations. Correspondent lenders can also fund mortgages or place the loan with another lender.

During the 2007-2008 recession, the correspondent lender's market collapsed. Dodd-Frank Wall Street Reform and Consumer Protection Act was passed in 2010 to provide risk mitigation in the financial markets and consumer protection. Correspondent lenders are now focusing on quality loan purchases and using technology for valuation tools, portfolio monitoring, and mortgage loan processing.

Lending professionals that are employees at a bank, savings and loan, or other institutions typically get a salary, with some incentive for loan production increases. Correspondent lenders make money by charging fees and mortgage brokers may charge fees or take a "cut" (yield spread premium or YSP) of the loan's interest from the lender. The lender that can provide instant approval with the lowest interest rate, lowest fees, fastest turnaround time (which means no paperwork, everything is done on the internet with e-sign), and highest probability of closing is the lender or mortgage banker you want.

While mortgage brokers can provide multiple lender offers, they typically cannot provide the approval assurance that going directly to a lender can afford.

Mortgage brokers offer the flexibility of being able to shop multiple lenders at once. But once they send the paperwork to the lender for underwriting approval, they have no control over the process.

Lenders may offer quicker turnarounds since they conduct underwriting themselves. This is not always true for loan officers at national banks — they often send their underwriting out of town to a central office.

Correspondent lenders is an excellent option, as they combine the flexibility of brokers and the processing speed and control of a lender.

Major Big Data Players

Major big data players who disseminate data to the market in different ways, according to the use for internal business purposes are:

1. Fannie Mae – available to their participants;

2. National Association of Homebuilders – membership and for-sale reports;

3. Appraisal Foundation – used for internal business decisions;

4. Costar / LoopNet – subscription for sale data;

5. Trulia / Zillow – free to everyone, with customized subscriptions;

6. Move /National Association of Realtors - free to everyone, with customized subscriptions;

7. Black Knight– subscription for sale data;

8. Realty Trac– subscription for sale data;

9. First American Title– subscription for sale data;

10. Corelogic– subscription for sale data; and

11. Enriched Data– subscription for sale data.

A handful of firms provide research commercial real estate data. Typically, data providers obtain their information from tax rolls, deeds and deeds of trust, which they supplement with contact information and other data, and verify and store in user-friendly, searchable databases. A complete dataset includes sales of residential and commercial properties with details on the brokers, buyers, sellers, lenders, management companies, tenants, physical and economic characteristics, and rent comparable with details on owners, management companies, brokers, and tenants, all of which they supplement with contact information. The data is typically utilized by:

- Real estate investors

- Property owners

- Leasing agents

- Real estate management companies

- Tenant and property service vendors (property insurance, title companies, pest control, office cleaning, etc.)

- Retail chains looking to expand

- Real estate appraisers

- Property tax consultants
- Real estate developers
- Media and communications providers
- Financial intermediaries (real estate brokers, banks, and mortgage lenders)
- Insurance companies
- Government agencies

Big data providers, like Enriched Data, collect the data electronically and then continuously verify it manually through other electronic searches and direct correspondence (phone calls, emails, surveys, etc.) with property owners, management companies, appraisers, leasing agents, etc. Professionals in the field, appraisers, brokers and mortgage bankers, using the data continually enrich the data with corrected or missing data points.

Other players in the space include CoStar, LoopNet, Digital Map Products, CoreLogic, Reis, and Real Capital Analytics. These business models are, for the most part, subscription-based services, which can be quite expensive with limited economies of scale for large subscribers (subscribers are required to obtain licenses for each employee and computer). In addition, typically any data obtained through the services cannot be re-sold.

FNMA Collateral Underwriter was introduced to the public by Fannie Mae on January 26, 2015, but had been used internally for years. Collateral Underwriter is a computer program designed to evaluate the quality and accuracy of residential real estate appraisals. It also identifies specific issues which appear to be a problem in an appraisal. While Collateral Underwriter has not received much attention in the general media, it has impacted lenders, borrowers and appraisers with regard to single-family loans. The best score is one and the lowest score is six.

The national rollout of Collateral Underwriter was on January 26, 2015 and it will intentionally have a dramatic impact on lenders for single-family housing. If Collateral Underwriter ranks an appraisal as one or two, there is no impact on the lender. A Collateral Underwriter ranking of three is considered neutral. However, when Collateral Underwriter ranks an appraisal as four or five, the lender is expected to review the appraisal closely to determine why the score is low. Fannie Mae acknowledges there will be false positives and that some poor quality appraisals will not be flagged by Collateral Underwriter.

Many industry participants believe if there is a sharp regional downturn in lending in one portion of the country, which leads to massive foreclosures, lenders who originated loans with a Collateral Underwriter ranking of four or five might be required to repurchase the loans even though the loan defaults are unrelated to the original appraisal. In practice, when a loan defaults, Fannie Mae likely looks at a variety of issues in deciding whether to require the lender to repurchase the loan. For the sake of simplicity and consistency, Collateral Underwriter scores of one and two will be considered passing, a score of three will be considered neutral, and a score of four or five will be considered to increase the lenders risk.

The impact on borrowers with regard to Collateral Underwriter include: 1) slower loan closings and 2) a lower number of loans closed. When lenders receive an appraisal which is ranked four or five by Collateral Underwriter, lenders will be expected to carefully review the appraisal to understand why the appraisal scored poorly. Some of the messages generated by Collateral Underwriter are vague and do not provide enough detail to clearly understand the basis of the poor score. For example, messages include:

- "There is a heightened risk of appraisal quality issues."
- "There is a heightened risk of overvaluation."
- "The condition rating is materially different than what has been reported by other appraisers."
- "The condition rating of "C3" conflicts with the reported age."

However, the appraiser and AMC will not have access to Collateral Underwriter and the report that it generates. A tagged report will allow the lender to return the appraisal to the appraiser and ask for changes to attempt to improve the Collateral Underwriter score. For example, one of the Collateral Underwriter flags is: "The appraiser-provided comparables are materially different than the model-selected comparables." In this case, a lender might ask an appraiser to look again and see if they can find comparable sales that are more similar to the subject. It could take several iterations for the appraiser to find comparable sales that effect a meaningful change in the Collateral Underwriter score.

No doubt, Collateral Underwriter increases the quality and professionalism of single-family appraisals. This occurs as appraisal decisions are data-driven instead of being made on more subjective factors. To stay away from its wrath, appraisers have to: 1) use more consistent and accurate data and 2) make more accurate adjustments. This will occur as appraisers gain access to tools to help them select the best comparable sales, make empirically-based adjustments and consistently use accurate data.

Collateral Underwriter will likely have the most significant impact on real estate appraisal in the U.S. in the next 20 years. While it will only affect single-family appraisal in the short term, it is likely to also effects commercial appraisal in the long term. The reason that Collateral Underwriter will also impact commercial real estate appraisals is because the benefit of using data which has been standardized by using quantitative grading will probably be adopted by commercial real estate appraisers. Being able to consistently rely upon commercial real estate sales based upon quality data will also allow commercial real estate lenders to utilize automatic valuation models to estimate the value of commercial real estate.

In the commercial real estate market:

- According to Borrell Assoc. in an August 2012 report, $23.7B in advertising will be spent on real estate advertising and 55% of that was to be spent on-line in 2012;

- Price per earnings ratios as high as 247x are evidenced by public companies providing commercial real estate information to professionals; and

- Real estate databases can provide business contact information that can be catered to buyers, sellers, owners, public companies, mortgage companies and vendors.

The market is not transparent to those without significant internal research capabilities. In an industry not known for adopting technology, companies that use big data and technology dominate pricing:

- Aggregation and the sale of unconfirmed tax roll data for just a few markets can cost over $200,000 annually, plus can come with resale restrictions of $0.42 to $14.40 for each property record resold. The few firms who have aggregated the data know the value proposition!

- LoopNet had 5.8 million registered members and 3.6 million unique visitors. Founded in 1995, three real estate companies funded the initial $3M (those investors also were huge subscribers), with Goldman Sachs funding over $20M in 1999. LoopNet merged with another company in 2001 and in 2003 had its first profitable year. In 2006, LoopNet had its first initial public offering and was purchased for over $865M by Costar in April 2012. The price equates to a 31% premium of the stock price, and JP Morgan funded $415M in a term loan, $50M in credit facility and the rest was 0.03702 shares of Costar common stock. Annualized in 2012, NOI is $9.6M, suggesting an 83 P/E Ratio.

As of 2/11/2013, Big Data real estate sector participants had the following financial characteristics:

Name	Ticker	Revenues	EBITDA	P/E	Market Cap (Millions)	Market Cap Revenues
Zillow	Z	102.4	11.95	208.62	1,210	11.73
Trulia	TRLA	51.00	(3.27)	NM	448	12.10
CoStar	CSGP	316.02	62.61	246.8	2,710	8.60
CoreLogic	CLGX	1,500.00	295.13	40.2	2,810	1.85
Move	MOVE	193.76	17.94	92.5	383	1.95
REIS	REIS	29.63	5.75	NM	159	5.28

Look up the tickers now and you will see substantial enhancement in market capitalization throughout this sector.

Data Integrity

Data integrity is essential in preparing quality appraisals. Appraisers who have database accessibility to allow them to analyze the data integrity in their appraisals is a key to solidifying our financial systems. Factors involving data integrity include accuracy with regard to the fields of data. It would be very helpful if there was a common database all appraisers could use that has the quality, condition, view and location factors. It would be even more helpful if it tracked sales price, square feet, land area and similar factors.

The first element of data integrity is whether the appraiser is using accurate data for the subject property and comparable sales for primary fields of data such as sales price, square feet of living area, quality, condition, location, view, and age. Quality, condition, location and view will be described by the letters QCLV. Since QCLV is subjective, it is difficult to impossible for an individual appraiser to use it consistently between appraisals without a database for comparison. Other fields of data are much easier to quantify such as sales price, square feet of living area, and age. Consistently using the same QCLV factors between appraisals will be difficult to impossible without having a software tool to help guide the appraiser. The appraiser who also has feedback on the factors being used by other appraisers is much less likely to have appraisals kicked back due to Collateral Underwriter scores of four or five.

Appraisers need a tool to help them evaluate whether their rankings for QCLV is similar to the rankings used in prior appraisals and to the rankings being used by other appraisers. This requires a database that includes data from the appraiser's prior appraisals as well as data from other appraiser's appraisals.

The cost approach is another area where data integrity is a factor. Antidotal reports indicate that many appraisers simply use a typical number such is $60 per square foot or $80 per square foot as the replacement cost for homes. Empirical data suggests that it is not clear if the replacement cost is correctly calculated by commercial and residential appraisers. Appraisers need to seek a quantitative basis for the replacement, level of depreciation, and land value.

Comparable Sale Selection

Real estate appraisal has been described as a combination of art and science. The process of selecting comparable sales would fall more into the art than science, based on how appraisers have typically selected comparable sales. Collateral Underwriter is attempting to create a wholesale change by making selection of comparable sales a quantitative process involving less judgment.

Comparable sale selection is most complex when a neighborhood is not homogeneous. Selecting comparable sales in a large, active homogeneous suburban neighborhood is relatively simple by comparison. Sales will generally be similar with regard to quality, condition, location, view and age. In newer neighborhoods, the quality and condition of homes is likely to be similar. However, in older subdivisions where remodeling has occurred, there will likely be more differences in quality and condition between homes.

The process of selecting sales in homogeneous neighborhoods has typically not involved any quantitative analysis. Sales are selected based upon their physical characteristics, location and time of sale, with secondary consideration given to supporting the actual sales price if the property is selling.

Appraisal education has historically taught that the most comparable sales are those with the lowest level of gross adjustments. However, some industry leaders suggest that sales with lowest adjustments are not necessarily better than sales with high adjustments. It is not clear how to interpret this. Until additional information becomes available, appraisers are encouraged to use comparable sales with the lowest gross adjustments, with emphasis on location, date of sale, and physical similarities. But appraisers must also factor in location as being the most important variable in most cases.

Quantitative Adjustments

Most residential appraisers have not used regression analysis and matched-pairs' analysis as a basis for making adjustments between comparable sales. It is clear using comparative analysis tools allows appraisers to consider quantitative data in making adjustments. For homes, using a per square foot adjustment for living area variation between the subject and the comparable is a key variable. A graph displayed by Fannie Mae representative Robert Murphy at a recent presentation showed that the median size adjustments are typically only about ten to twenty percent of the sales price per square foot. It is fair to say the audience was shocked at the disparity between adjustments for size and the sales prices per square foot.

The ideal option for appraisers is to use a form-fill software program that integrates both regression analysis and a matched pair sales analysis. This would provide the appraiser with information on both the level of adjustment and the reliability of the proposed adjustment for a regression analysis. The matched pair sales data would provide the data including the level of adjustment and the number of records used to generate the proposed adjustment.

Reconciliation

Reconciliation is the final step in the appraisal process. It involves evaluating the quality and quantity of data available for each of the approaches to appraisal. Real estate appraisal typically uses the sales comparison approach, cost approach, and income approach. However, in practice, residential appraisal uses the sales comparison approach with little or no consideration given to the cost approach, unless the house is new or less than five years old. The income approach is used infrequently and then typically only for rental homes or investment properties.

Since the cost approach is given only token consideration, and the income approach is rarely used in residential appraisals, the heart of the reconciliation process is really done by concluding to a value in the sales comparison approach. Conceptually, real estate appraisal can generate either a range of value or a pinpoint value.

The final value after reconciliation should be consistent with both the adjusted values for the comparable sales and within a reasonable range of the cost approach and/or income approach values. There are companies that offer reports that include a quantitative analysis of the subject property and the comparable sales in the area. However, preparing an appraisal using multiple computer programs will be time consuming:

- Use a program to first analyze the comparable sales in the area;
- Go to the multiple listing service to pull more detailed information on the comparable sales;
- Type the information on the sales into the form-fill program; and
- Consult the quantitative report while making adjustments for the comparable sales.

Today, the appraisal process is opaque as the lender simply receives the comparable sales selected by the appraiser with no data on sales not selected. The lender does not know if the appraiser has selected the best sales or simply selected sales to support the value. Based on appraisal reports submitted to the FBI for investigation, it appears that appraisal fraud is limited and atypical. Hence, appraisal fraud has not been a serious or widespread problem. Unfortunately, due to the media reports regarding appraisal fraud, the perception of fraud exceeds the actual problem. The vast majority of appraisers will be relieved to have fraudulent appraisers excluded from the industry. However, there is the need to improve the appraisal quality by forcing the appraiser to think carefully about which comparable sales are best for the appraisal and then finding a tool to do qualitative analysis. Further, few appraisers use quantitative analysis to make adjustments. While appraisers will be unenthusiastic about both the oversight on selecting comparable sales and using a tool to determine quantitative adjustments, the result will be better quality appraisal reports.

Where Do I Get Commercial Data?

Enriched Data (national) Enriched Data is the largest enriched base in the country, used by mortgage bankers, mortgage brokers, real estate brokers, property owners, sellers of properties, investors, lenders of all types, and businesses that provide services to real estate confirmed commercial and residential information. Detailed contact data (phone, email, address, LinkedIn) confirmed with the actual party is the key to having reliable contact data. The company has databased every property, 200M+ people active in the real estate space and updates any sale, loan, encumbrance or other event as close to that event as possible.

Proprietary programs and applications allow subscribers to get the data they want, in a manner that makes them more efficient, more money. Sales Force, Goldkey, Outlook and even Act are uploaded with thousands of client contacts weekly. Investors can view listings, sales, market reports, view standardized national tax roll data and run a sales comparison approach on properties within a few minutes.

The company is also changing the way municipal bond underwriters price bonds where real estate tax is the basis for bond repayment. Looking at up to 12 year economic trends in a market, like house appreciation, foreclosure percentages, changes in assessments, changes in number of sales and other local and regional factors provides economic insight previously not available. And these tools are changing an industry that has not changed in decades.

Enriched Data's foundation spun off from O'Connor & Associates database, the largest tax consultant in the U.S.

- **CoStar** (national) Provides commercial real estate research and information services in the US, UK, and France, covering data on space available for lease, comparable sales information, tenant information, properties for sale, information about industry professionals and their business relationships, and provides internet marketing services, data integration, and industry news. The company employs hundreds of researchers. It also provides market research and analysis for commercial real estate investors and lenders, portfolio and debt management and reporting, and real estate and lease management including lease administration and abstraction services. Services are typically distributed to clients under annual, automatically renewing, subscription-based license agreements.

CoStar has reasonable quality data but many of its clients are displeased for three related reasons: 1) CoStar is rigid in requiring a license for each potential user, 2) their pricing is quite high ($300 to $1200 per user per month), and 3) there is a perception that the data does not merit the price. However, most users believe there is no viable option, particularly for office leasing data and comparable sales data in non-disclosure states.

CoStar is publicly traded (CSGP) with a multi-billion dollar market capitalization, with a PE ratio of well over 100.

- **LoopNet** (national) Operates an online commercial real estate listing service, containing more than $425 billion of property available for sale and 6.3 billion square feet of property available for lease. LoopNet is like a multiple listing service for commercial properties, brokers post their commercial property listing on the website for a fee, and subscribers access those commercial listings.

LoopNet, which was a publicly traded company, was purchased by CoStar in 2012 for $883 million, a 31% premium to the LoopNet's market capitalization.

- **Digital Map Products** (national) Provides property and geospatial data, visual analysis, market and environmental data, aerial imagery, drawing tools, spatial search features, and map-based interfaces, and allows users to create custom maps with drawing tools, labels, images and imported data. Digital Map also provides data to governments and businesses through re-licensing agreements with data and information companies, acting as a central resource for managing licensing contracts and providing support. Third-party data includes county parcel data, property ownership from county clerk sales records, assessor tax maps, street centerline databases (for use in geo-coding applications, street names, and points of interest information), stock aerial photography, natural hazards (detailing FEMA flood zones, fire zones, etc.), and environmental hazards (Superfund sites, leaking tanks, etc.)

- **CoreLogic** (national) Manages a database of property, mortgage and consumer information in the US, UK, Australia, and New Zealand. Manages geospatial parcel data, property tax data, flood and disaster data, criminal background records, eviction information, consumer credit information, MLS listings, and mortgage-backed and asset-backed securities information within the US. The company also provides automated valuation models and mortgage origination and default management systems including property tax and settlement services, as well as automotive credit reporting.

CoreLogic announced its intention to acquire Marshall & Swift/Boeckh and Dataquick Information Systems in July 2013, for $661 million. Marshall & Swift/Boeckh provides residential and commercial property valuations, DataQuick Information Systems manages a property data and provides analytics and credit and flood services. CoreLogic is publicly traded (CLGX) with a multi-billion dollar market capitalization.

- **REIS** (national) Manages a database of apartment, office, retail, warehouse, distribution, and self-storage properties, including rents, rent discounts and other concessions, vacancy rates, lease terms, property sales, new construction listings, property valuation estimates, tenant improvement allowances, and operating expenses. In addition, Reis processes multiple data sources, including public filings databases, tax assessor records, deed transfers, planning boards, and local, regional and national publications and commercial real estate websites. Reis provides reports containing research data and forecasts, as well as analytical tools. Services are typically distributed to clients under annual subscription-based user agreements. Reis only researches a subset of the building and sales. While they have helpful statistical data, their dataset is not comprehensive. This is a serious problem for transactional professionals.

  Reis is publicly traded (REIS) with a multi-million dollar market capitalization.

- **Real Capital Analytics** (national) Manages global transactional information for property sales and financing including related transaction parties (buyers, sellers, any joint venture partners, advisors, lenders and brokers), and publishes Global Capital Trends and US Capital Trends, and regularly reports on distressed commercial property trends.

- **ALN Apartment Data** (national) Manages a database of apartment information within the Texas, Georgia, Florida, Arizona, Nevada, and Arkansas markets, and provides a web-based apartment locator with access to market data and statistical analyses.

- **Pierce-Eislen** (national) Provides property owner and managing entity contact information, including individual property and general market conditions, photographs, physical characteristics, prior sales, rental history, and property ownership/management details.

Valuation Metrics in the Sector

Competitor	Ticker	2012 Revenue	2012 Net Income	2012 Operating Margin	Market Cap (*as of* 12/31/12)
CoStar	CSGP	$350 Million	$10 Million	5.3%	$2.6 Billion
CoreLogic	CLGX	$1.6 Billion	$112 Million	14.3%	$2.6 Billion
Reis	REIS	$31 Million	$(4) Million	9.7%	$141 Million

Real estate and data are at a crossroads where new technology applications are needed to effectively process big data into reasonable solutions; making industry professionals more efficient. In an industry still needing to show transparency and slow to adapt to technology, we expect a faster transition in the future than the past in adopting big data solutions.

SOCIO-ECONOMIC DECISIONS WILL MOVE POPULATIONS

Big data and technology will allow each of us to look at decision making different in the future.

Who would have thought that 37,000,000 names of subscriber's using a website to explore relationships outside their marriage would be published worldwide? Human characteristics of taking on different levels of risk to get rewards vary among all of us. Some are willing to take great risks to achieve personal and economic satisfaction. Others tend to stay in structured environments that provide minimal volatility in personal and economic rewards.

The same can be said about homeownership and real estate investment. Some wealthy homeowners acquired huge estates and multiple homes, only to find a lack of personal satisfaction with owning "large spaces" that are never used. We developed a phrase called "island syndrome" in 2006 when the world's wealthy people were purchasing private islands. The cost was typically not in the price of the island, but in the cost of putting facilities and homes on those islands that also required upkeep. Typically, islands in the $2,000,000 to $10,000,000 range can require a minimum of $5,000,000 to build docks, air landing strips, utility systems, homes, caretaker facilities, etc. This can take years, and once buyers spent time on their island, they became so lonely that they sold the island within three to five years.

Commercial investors tend to be a little more structured in their decision-making. But is there a way to measure all purchase opportunities within a given land use code and pricing range? How does purchasing properties at auction vary from purchasing in a competitive marketing environment through a property listed in a Multiple Listing Service?

In a seller's market, a good quality house in a great location will incur multiple offers in the first few days of the MLS posting, many times, above market pricing. Then the seller has to worry about the appraiser coming up with a lower value than the pending price. The lender typically loans on the sale price or appraised value, whichever is lower. Lack of technology and limited big data-processing capabilities in the appraisal business causes significant issues in a quickly appreciating market. So both sellers and buyers have legitimate concerns that the appraiser will not "hit" the offer or accepted price in a fast appreciating real estate market.

Most investors will agree, you make money on the BUY side (price < value). Buying properties below market establishes a baseline book value that allows you to:

1. Resell at a discount to market value if funds are needed quickly;

2. Achieve higher yields in an appreciating market;

3. Withstand a real estate market that starts to depreciate than other owners.

While there is nothing wrong with buying at market value (price = value), the herd mentality of all competitive properties also being at market value requires your property to be better managed, better maintained and/or uniquely in demand in order to achieve better than average returns.

Neilsen's Prizm platform uses homeowner segmentation based on socio-economic characteristics and the homeowners' lifestyle. Every homeowner is segments into one of three lifestyle group categories.

Code	LG	Lifestage Group

01	Y1	Y1 Midlife Success
02	Y2	Y2 Young Achievers
03	Y3	Y3 Striving Singles
04	F1	F1 Accumulated Wealth
05	F2	F2 Young Accumulators
06	F3	F3 Mainstream Families
07	F4	F4 Sustaining Families
08	M1	M1 Affluent Empty Nesters
09	M2	M2 Conservative Classics
10	M3	M3 Cautious Couples
11	M4	M4 Sustaining Seniors

Source: Neilsen

Younger years are typically new homeowners entering the real estate market. They are not typically single-head-of-households unless they have had some economic success. They are using their first purchase of typically a smaller home as a staging platform for moving-up, once they build equity.

Family-life years are cohabitates that typically require at least three-bedrooms, two-baths and a central dining area. Families come together for food. Food brings warmth, comfort and a loving interaction that transcends conflicts and differences. For generations, family life has been the central core of American financial and social security.

Mature years are those homeowners and renters that have to budget. They are adversely affected by big swings in utility, insurance and property tax payments. Historically, they loved home ownership, but in the retirement years, they are not sitting on the front porch in rocking chairs, but traveling and looking for employment and entrepreneurial opportunities that can supplement their social security and retirement savings.

However, changes in social interaction in newer generations are changing the way families interact and many are opting for single or dual apartment living. The young generations who opt to live long distances from their families are actually motivating seniors to relocate at retirement to be close to their children. These trends affect real estate demand and the smart real estate investors should recognize if these trends are relevant in the market they are targeting.

Whether buying a house to live in, or buying one for investment, there are new ways to look at home acquisitions. Know not only the real estate, but also the characteristics of those who live in the house and the neighborhood.

HOW TO ANALYZE DEMAND IN REAL ESTATE

This discussion outlines methods of analyzing demand for various property types: residential, retail, office and multifamily / apartments. Let us go back to year-end 2008, when the financial crisis in America was in full swing and use an unnamed smaller U.S. city to analyze demand. Upon completion of the analysis and some forward-looking projections based on known factors as of December 2008, we can analyze current inventory and demand to see how accurate the projections were.

This discussion will also include cost analysis, funding sources, competitive market analysis, financial feasibility and other factors involved in a proposed Riverfront project in a city situated in Middle America. The Riverfront project is planned for entertainment, hotel, marina, office, retail, apartment and for-sale housing inventory. We are using excel-based demand and supply models. If the reader is interested, please contact the authors for a free copy. While there are other methods to measure supply and demand, these models have been proven reliable over decades of use around the U.S. and the world.

The intended land uses should:

1. Have the ability to capture a percentage of demand from existing community growth generators, organic growth from births and expanding employers; and

2. Have the ability to capture new demand from sources that currently are not being generated within the community.

Demand comes from:

- Developers catering to baby boomers (mature years) looking for a quality of life in retirement and younger years that have achieved some above average economic income stability looking for a live, work, and play environment;

- Retailers – both specialty and general commercial;

- Hoteliers;

- Office users – primarily oriented to white collar employment;

- Marina operators;

- Condominium, townhouse and apartment developers; and

- Recreational and sports developers and operators – both indoors and outdoors

This analysis will provide research data and analysis relative to property build out to include:

- Preliminary Land Use "Bubble Plan;"

- Project Overview;

- Existing Hard, Soft and Intellectual Assets;

- Competitive Market Overview/Comparable Riverfront and Downtown Development Projects;

- Office Market Analysis;

- Apartment Market Analysis;

- Residential Market Overview;

- Baby Boomer Demand;

- Retail Market Analysis;

- Potential Users and Tenants Market Analysis; and

- Need for CC&Rs and Homeowner's Association documents to supplement Zoning.

Population and employment based demand models will help future business determine how they can best fit into the integrated mixed-use development. The next phase of the process will include the following documentation while specific uses and investors are targeted for the riverfront development:

- Preliminary Marina Overview and Highlights;

- Preliminary Construction Cost Estimates;

- Lodging Market Supply and Demand/Tourism/Potential Hotel Brands;

- Bulk Commercial/Retail Parcel Sales Analysis;

- Estimated Hotel, Condominium, Apartment, Commercial, and Marina Construction Costs;

- Hotel, Condominium, Apartment, Commercial, and Marina Operating Pro Formas;

- Bulk Hotel, Condominium, Apartment and Commercial Land Sales Analysis;

- Users Market Analysis;

- Total Property Project Sales and Cash Flow Projections; and

- Government Incentives and Initiatives.

Office Market Analysis

The local office market contains 103,388 square feet of space. Based on an economist's employment projections, white collar (excludes agricultural, military and other non-office related businesses) employment allocations and an estimated 85% office space occupancy level, the following reflects 5-year projections on occupancy and demand:

Year		Total Employed	Employment Growth %	Annual Workers Added	Office Inventory	Occupied Office Space	SF/ Employee	Direct Annual Absorption (SF)	Direct Available	Annual Supply Change
Actual										
Year-end	2008	125,212	0.27%	335	103,388	87,880	0.7	0	15.0%	N/A
Projected										
Year-end	2009	125,547	-0.62%	335	103,388	88,115	0.7	235	14.8%	0
Year-end	2010	124,765	0.85%	(783)	103,388	87,566	0.7	(549)	15.3%	0
Year-end	2011	125,822	2.10%	1,057	103,388	88,308	0.7	742	14.6%	0
Year-end	2012	128,466	2.05%	2,644	103,388	90,164	0.7	1,856	12.8%	0
Year-end	2013	131,101	2.05%	2,635	103,388	92,013	0.7	1,849	11.0%	0
5 Year Average			1.29%	1,178			0.7	827	13.7%	0
5 Year Total			6.43%	5,889				4,133		0
Notes:	Projections for employment growth based on local economists projections.									

As noted, there was 103,388 square feet of office supply in 2008 with a 15% vacancy rate. Over the next five years, total employed increased from 125,547 to 131,101 employed, a 1.29% average annual increase and an increase of 5,889 workers over the next five years. If office inventory remains static at 103,388 square feet, and using the current 0.7 square feet of occupied office space per employee (occupied office space divided by total employed), then occupied office space should increase from 87,880 to 92,013 by year end 2013. Direct available vacancy will fall from the current 15.0% to 11.0 and 4,133 square feet of total direct absorption will be evidenced, likely not sufficient to support significant office development in this community.

However, relocations of businesses that demand office space from outside the community would significantly change the demand projections. The attractiveness of a riverfront development is unique to the region. Could a Tier 3 city, (typically less than 1 million population) with a riverfront development, be strategically situated to attract Class A office users that would otherwise not have considered relocating? Although not large in scale, CEOs around the country are in fact viewing the lifestyle and cost of living when making relocation decisions. In order to attract a small to medium sized company to the quality-of-life aspects of a Tier 3 city are easier today than ever. The internet allows employees to connect to the world and technology applications provide efficiencies that allow quality of life and quality of employment opportunities in smaller communities.

This analysis suggests there is some risk inherent in building an office building at this site. Rather, pre-leasing with an anchor office tenant would be a much better alternative. If office development were undertaken, a building around 4,133 square feet is recommended, taking six to 12 months to building and leasing over the next 48 to 54 months, if regional demand is not a factor. However, a confident developer would push to see of existing office tenants with leases coming due in the next 12 to 36 months would be interested in occupying the space.

Residential Market Analysis

By the end of 2008, there was a substantial decline in home sales in many parts of the country. This downturn was preceded by strong appreciation in home prices. This appreciation outpaced income levels and affordability was a real issue in many areas of the country. Cheap money in the form of low interest rates, minimal, if any, down payments and seller-paid closing costs formed the perfect storm. And home ownership percentages increased, fast.

Wall Street firms jumped into the market, supplementing the funds government regulated entities provided, such as Fannie Mae and other Government Sponsored Agencies who were previously the main buyers of mortgages from lenders. But when Wall Street investors entered the market for buying real estate loans and providing sophisticated investment vehicles in the form of mortgage backed securities to the buyers of those pooled mortgages, then the risk profile of the housing market was exacerbated beyond even the leading economists' expectation. Increasing home prices coupled with new builder inventory fed a buyer market that had a significant percentage of investor purchases, in some markets over 20% of the new housing stock.

Foreclosures then began to show up. The 1% to 3% reserves set aside for losses quickly became known to these investors. Wall Street could no longer sell these sophisticated investments to lay investors who did little to evaluate the underlying risk of the asset. Housing prices across America fell and the combination of record high foreclosures almost collapsed the U.S. economy.

In normalized market conditions, residential real estate markets tend to have local demand drivers. Many smaller market areas survived the downturn much better than some large cities. Most Tier 3 cities that did not experience double digit annual appreciation had a reduction in demand for homes, but it was not as devastating as it was in large metropolitan areas. Most of the smaller U.S. communities did not have double-digit appreciation during the years prior to the nation's financial crisis. This graft is a summary of the smaller U.S. communities relative to housing costs as a percentage of income levels:

Housing Statistics								
	12-Month SF Permits	12-Month Total Permits	Total Permits / Peak Permits	1-Yr Growth	Affordability 1-Yr Growth Rate	Unemp Rate	Median Home Price	Housing Costs / Income	Housing Cycle Barometer
1 Saginaw	116	138	14%	-2,700	-3.20%	11.80%	$43,606	9%	0.1
2 Youngstown	310	450	24%	-12,100	-5.10%	12.80%	$63,778	12%	0.1
3 Toledo	561	1,008	24%	-18,100	-5.60%	12.00%	$81,130	13%	0.2
4 Lansing	225	308	10%	-9,700	-4.30%	9.60%	$81,438	13%	0
5 Fort Smith	505	723	55%	-1,400	-1.10%	7.00%	$78,906	14%	0
6 Grand Rapids	830	876	17%	-20,100	-5.20%	10.50%	$83,076	14%	0.1
7 Fort Myers	1,003	1,238	4%	-19,500	-8.80%	11.90%	$85,000	14%	0
8 Cleveland	1,942	2,284	29%	-48,100	-4.50%	9.00%	$93,884	14%	0.2
9 Wheeling	36	36	12%	-400	-0.60%	8.60%	$77,026	15%	0
10 Texarkana	289	325	39%	-200	-0.30%	5.20%	$78,484	15%	0

Affordability and quality of life will be the two major factors that the baby boom generation will look to as they attempt to find retirement locations. And those locations can also be found attractive to millennials. With outdoor and recreational opportunities not found in big cities, millennials expect to have more social time and a live, work, play environment is right up their alley; while also being an attractive retirement location for baby boomers. Find markets attractive to both baby boomers and millennials and you have a winner!

Building Permits

Look to at least a 10-year construction trend in your market to determine the relative health of the new housing market. Let's take a look at a Tier 3 city's construction trends:

The Riverfront Site's Regional Single-Family Building Permits

	Number of Dwelling Units		Average Value per Dwelling Unit ($)	
Year	Units	Percent Change	Value	Percent Change
1998	610	-1	91,700	5
1999	517	-15	117,500	28
2000	431	-17	113,900	-3
2001	480	11	119,600	5
2002	602	25	115,500	-3
2003	651	8	120,300	4
2004	585	-10	126,700	5
2005	701	20	125,400	-1
2006	575	-18	124,100	-1
2007	732	27	123,000	-1

Source: U.S. Bureau of Census and Real Estate Center at Texas A&M University
Note: MSA data is based on 1999 MSA definitions.

Through the first half of 2009 permits have not seen any significant decline:

| | | Number of Dwelling Units | | Average Value per Dwelling Unit ($) | | |
| | | 12 Month | | | 12 Month | |
Date	Units	Total	Percent Change	Average Value	Average	Percent Change
2008-Jan	29	608	20	127,600	124,900	2
Feb	32	595	16	152,400	124,900	0
Mar	31	526	-9	136,300	129,500	6
Apr	35	506	-14	119,400	127,800	4
May	42	482	-21	179,000	134,100	10
Jun	35	456	-26	122,600	135,800	12
Jul	29	444	-25	210,800	139,300	15
Aug	23	392	-34	142,500	149,000	24
Sep	32	396	-32	157,000	149,400	23
Oct	21	384	-34	145,200	149,200	21
Nov	27	370	-39	116,900	147,800	20
Dec	17	353	-43	118,900	145,700	17
2009-Jan	24	348	-43	96,200	143,800	15
Feb	20	336	-44	146,500	143,100	15
Mar	29	334	-37	116,900	141,500	9
Apr	52	351	-31	124,100	141,100	10
May	27	336	-30	128,300	135,400	1

Source: U.S. Bureau of Census and Real Estate Center at Texas A&M University

As noted from a review of new-home construction in this market, it tended to weather the housing downturn many other parts of the country experienced. Trends like these are important to investors looking to long-term holds.

Affordability

By national home-price standards, the riverfront site area stacks up favorably on the affordability front. The following chart reflects home sales and average home pricing for the community.

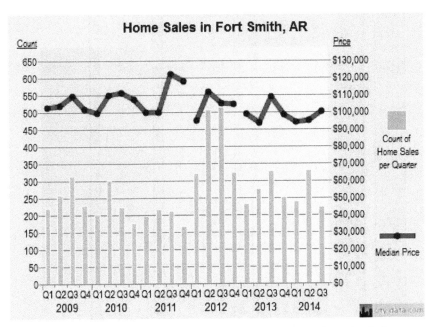

The Riverfront Site MLS Residential Housing Activity

Using the information provided by Precis, we have built projections based on housing and apartment demand through 2012.

Metropolitan Fort Smith
Residential Home and Apartment Absorption

	Historical							Projected Growth per Economists	Estimated 2008	Projected			
	2001	2002	2003	2004	2005	2006	2007			2009	2010	2011	2012
						Metropolitan Fort Smith							
Total Employment	117,141	115,740	115,377	116,864	119,738	123,246	125,212	6,889	125,547	124,765	125,822	128,466	131,101
Employment Growth (no. of jobs)		-1,402	-363	1,487	3,999	6,383	1,966		335	(783)	1,057	2,644	2,635
Percentage Growth		-1.20%	-0.31%	1.29%	3.42%	5.33%	1.60%		0.27%	-0.62%	0.85%	2.10%	2.05%
Average							1.88%						
Population - Fort Smith	275,521	277,232	278,569	280,380	281,748	285,598	289,693	17,423	291,060	296,525	300,269	304,116	307,116
Population Growth		1,711	1,337	1,811	2,368	3,850	3,095		3,367	3,465	3,744	3,847	3,001
Percentage Growth		0.62%	0.48%	0.65%	0.84%	1.34%	1.07%		1.16%	1.18%	1.25%	1.28%	0.99%
Average		0.82%	0.66%	0.88%	0.66%	0.78%	0.83%						
Summary of Housing & Lot Demand													
House Absorption/Permits	598	683	784	866	784	661	800	Proj.Total/Avg	503	284	686	740	714
Average	624	624	661	660	661	654	668						
			Housing Absorption based on:					Employment	168	(391)	529	755	753
								Population	842	866	749	769	600
								Moody's Proj.	501	377	419	696	790
Ratio - Employment Growth/House Absorption		-2.05	-0.49	2.27	5.10	9.66	2.46	2.00	2.00	2.00	2.00	3.50	3.50
Ratio - Population Growth/House Absorption		0.40	0.55	0.35	0.33	0.17	0.26	0.26	0.25	0.25	0.20	0.20	0.20
Apartment Absorption/Permits	129	360	227	282	287	147	305	Proj.Total/Avg	166	84	157	244	238
Average		240	235	235	241	225	237		248	89	10	22	63
Ratio - Apt. Absorption/Home Absorption	22.8%	51.2%	30.9%	35.4%	34.1%	22.2%	38.1%	Moody's Proj.	33.0%	33.0%	33.0%	33.0%	33.0%
Average							33.6%	33.0%					
Apartment Demand as % of Total Demand	18.6%	33.9%	23.6%	26.2%	25.4%	18.2%	27.6%		24.8%	24.8%	24.8%	24.8%	24.8%
Average							24.8%						
Total House and Apartment Demand	686	1,033	661	887	1,061	808	1,105		670	378	762	984	950

Note: Historical population figures taken from Claritas; employment from Moody's Economy.com

Forecasted Absorption

In forecasting absorption for the planning-area parcel, we have relied on historical trends, as well as future projections for population growth within the subject's market area. We have provided a demographic study of the market area (considered a 5-mile radius of the riverfront site) in order to estimate future demand. These projections will be used as the basis for future demand relative to housing.

One method for forecasting absorption is through the projection of employment and population growth. Household growth, which is ultimately a function of an area's economy, will provide our foundation for housing absorption.

FULL DEMOGRAPHIC PROFILE
62 NORTH B STREET, FORT SMITH, ARKANSAS
FORT SMITH, ARKANSAS

	1.0 MILE	5.0 MILES	10.0 MILES	FORT SMITH	SEBASTIAN COUNTY, AR	ARKANSAS
Population						
2013 Projection	2,555	68,742	144,552	86,929	126,360	2,966,499
2008 Estimate	2,578	67,138	138,119	84,238	121,902	2,851,028
2000 Census	2,682	65,060	128,348	80,268	115,071	2,673,400
1990 Census	2,456	61,822	113,407	73,132	99,590	2,350,725
Growth 2008 - 2013	-0.18%	0.47%	0.91%	0.63%	0.72%	0.80%
Growth 2000 - 2008	-0.49%	0.39%	0.92%	0.61%	0.72%	0.81%
Growth 1990 - 2000	0.88%	0.51%	1.25%	0.94%	1.46%	1.29%
2008 Est. Population by Age	2,578	67,138	138,119	84,238	121,902	2,851,028
Age 0 - 4	7.97%	8.14%	7.65%	7.96%	7.75%	6.86%
Age 5 - 9	7.30%	7.49%	7.33%	7.41%	7.30%	6.64%
Age 10 - 14	6.82%	7.03%	7.11%	6.94%	6.97%	6.68%
Age 15 - 17	4.12%	3.75%	4.13%	3.85%	4.12%	4.15%
Age 18 - 20	4.50%	3.64%	3.63%	3.59%	3.60%	4.31%
Age 21 - 24	6.54%	4.61%	4.75%	4.55%	4.64%	5.35%
Age 25 - 34	16.95%	14.05%	13.55%	13.56%	13.03%	13.37%
Age 35 - 44	14.64%	13.50%	13.72%	13.59%	13.72%	13.20%
Age 45 - 49	6.72%	6.64%	7.18%	7.07%	7.29%	7.02%
Age 50 - 54	5.90%	6.39%	6.79%	6.82%	6.94%	6.68%
Age 55 - 59	4.85%	5.88%	6.22%	6.25%	6.42%	6.27%
Age 60 - 64	3.78%	4.84%	5.01%	4.99%	5.19%	5.27%
Age 65 - 74	5.38%	6.84%	6.80%	6.76%	6.88%	7.50%
Age 75 - 84	3.01%	4.82%	4.24%	4.47%	4.18%	4.69%
Age 85 and over	1.54%	2.36%	1.88%	2.18%	1.98%	2.02%
Households						
2013 Projection	836	27,187	56,607	34,624	49,217	1,184,953
2008 Estimate	860	26,759	54,094	33,718	47,678	1,129,118
2000 Census	927	26,267	50,271	32,398	45,300	1,042,696
1990 Census	1,014	25,569	44,076	29,746	39,298	891,179
Growth 2008 - 2013	-0.57%	0.32%	0.91%	0.53%	0.64%	0.97%
Growth 2000 - 2008	-0.93%	0.23%	0.92%	0.50%	0.64%	1.00%
Growth 1990 - 2000	-0.89%	0.27%	1.32%	0.86%	1.43%	1.58%
2008 Est. Households by Household Income	860	26,759	54,094	33,718	47,678	1,129,118
Income Less than $15,000	38.75%	22.13%	17.94%	18.87%	16.68%	17.81%
Income $15,000 - $24,999	20.51%	17.39%	14.81%	15.27%	14.50%	14.23%
Income $25,000 - $34,999	12.40%	15.61%	13.98%	14.41%	14.24%	13.53%
Income $35,000 - $49,999	9.78%	16.87%	18.07%	16.62%	17.69%	17.37%
Income $50,000 - $74,999	11.09%	14.52%	17.39%	16.30%	17.79%	18.45%
Income $75,000 - $99,999	4.81%	6.13%	8.22%	7.87%	8.69%	8.70%
Income $100,000 - $149,999	2.14%	4.28%	6.22%	6.28%	6.67%	6.62%
Income $150,000 - $249,999	0.13%	1.89%	2.13%	2.73%	2.31%	2.23%
Income $250,000 - $499,999	0.39%	0.73%	0.87%	1.12%	0.97%	0.78%
Income $500,000 and more	0.00%	0.45%	0.38%	0.53%	0.46%	0.27%
2008 Est. Average Household Income	$30,315	$45,189	$50,945	$52,694	$53,084	$51,205
2008 Est. Median Household Income	$20,424	$31,715	$37,718	$36,308	$38,886	$38,828
2008 Est. Per Capita Income	$10,853	$18,324	$20,172	$21,348	$20,992	$20,482

Previously it was demonstrated that population and employment growth supported 1,646 to 2,984 future housing permits and 760 apartment permits from 2009 to 2012. We used demographic projections to reflect the potential "capture" ratios for a 5-mile radius of the riverfront site:

Projected Household Growth for Subject Area (5-Mile Radius) Per Claritas					
	2009	2010	2011	2012	2013
Sebastian County Households	47,983	48,290	48,599	48,910	49,223
Subject Area Percentage	55.9%	55.8%	55.6%	55.4%	55.2%
Subject Area Households	26,845	26,931	27,017	27,103	27,190
Subject Area Annual Household Growth	86	86	86	86	87
Building Permits	284	565	740	714	714
Subject Area Capture Ratio	30.1%	15.2%	11.6%	12.1%	12.1%

We then qualified the population based on affordability of potential qualifying purchasers that could afford housing at riverfront site:

Qualifying Purchasers			
Home Price	95% Mortgage	Annual PITI	Indicated Income
$180,000	$171,000	$14,378	$47,925
to			
$400,000	$380,000	$31,950	$106,500

With $180,000 to $400,000 projected housing prices, we can then use household growth and income qualifying criteria to determine potential demand for the proposed "for sale" housing at the riverfront site:

Total Market by Income Strata (5-Mile Radius)					
	2011	2012	2013	2014	2015
Household Growth	86	86	86	86	87
2009 Demand for Competitive Priced Homes	28.0%	28.0%	28.0%	28.0%	28.0%
Total Annual Market by Income Strata	24	24	24	24	24

Because not all households who have the potential to purchase a home will actually purchase that home, we have allocated future demand between potential home buyers and renters on a quarterly basis:

Projected Quarterly Absorption of Subject Lots															
Quarter 1	2	3	4	1	2	3	4	1	2	3	4	1	2	3	4
Year 2011	2011	2011	2011	2012	2012	2012	2012	2013	2013	2013	2013	2014	2014	2014	2014
Total Market by Income Strata	6	6	6	6	6	6	6	6	6	6	6	6	6	6	6
Single Family Preference - 5 Yr Avg. 71.7%	71.7%	71.7%	71.7%	71.7%	71.7%	71.7%	71.7%	71.7%	71.7%	71.7%	71.7%	71.7%	71.7%	71.7%	71.7%
Total Market for Development	4	4	4	4	4	4	4	4	4	4	4	4	4	4	4
Estimated Capture Rate 50.0%	50.0%	50.0%	50.0%	55.0%	55.0%	55.0%	55.0%	65.0%	65.0%	65.0%	65.0%	75.0%	75.0%	75.0%	75.0%
Quarterly Potential Lot/Home Sales	2	2	2	2	2	2	2	2	3	3	3	3	3	3	3
Supplemental Demand - External	4	4	4	4	4	4	4	4	4	4	4	4	4	4	4
Retirement Demand	1	1	1	1	1	1	1	1	1	1	1	1	1	1	1
Total Absorption	7	7	7	7	7	7	7	7	7	7	7	8	8	8	8
Cumulative Absorption 117															

Projected Quarterly Absorption of Subject Multifamily Units															
Quarter 1	2	3	4	1	2	3	4	1	2	3	4	1	2	3	4
Year 2011	2011	2011	2011	2012	2012	2012	2012	2013	2013	2013	2013	2014	2014	2014	2014
Total Market by Income Strata	6	6	6	6	6	6	6	6	6	6	6	6	6	6	6
Multifamily Preference - 5 Yr Avg. 28.3%	28.3%	28.3%	28.3%	28.3%	28.3%	28.3%	28.3%	28.3%	28.3%	28.3%	28.3%	28.3%	28.3%	28.3%	28.3%
Total Market for Development	2	2	2	2	2	2	2	2	2	2	2	2	2	2	2
Estimated Capture Rate 35.0%	35.0%	35.0%	35.0%	40.0%	40.0%	40.0%	40.0%	50.0%	50.0%	50.0%	50.0%	60.0%	60.0%	60.0%	60.0%
Quarterly Potential MF Unit Demand	1	1	1	1	1	1	1	1	1	1	1	1	1	1	1
Supplemental Demand - External	4	4	4	4	4	4	4	4	4	4	4	4	4	4	4
Potential Age Restricted Demand	1	1	1	1	1	1	1	1	1	1	1	1	1	1	1
Total Absorption	5	5	5	5	5	5	5	6	6	6	6	6	6	6	6
Cumulative Absorption 87															

After projecting housing lot demand, we then isolated demand for rental housing in multifamily units. The preference between single family (lot absorption) and multifamily housing allocation is allocated based on percentages of current housing stock. The estimated capture rate is the analyst's way of allocating demand between the various housing types.

We used three categories of demand:

1. Quarterly Potential Lot/Home Sales - derived directly from economists' household growth projections;

2. Supplemental Demand – External – estimated based on the riverfront site ability to attract potential homeowners and renters from outside the community; and

3. Retirement Demand – 55+ age categories that are not affected by employment projections.

Based on these projections, the riverfront site should be able to attract the following levels of demand:

1. Condos and townhomes as a result of home ownership demand; and

2. Apartments as a result of rental home demand.

Since this analysis was originally conducted in 2008, let us see how close the model came to reality:

Actual City Permits

Year	Single Family	2-, 3&4, 5+Unit Multi-Family
2012	229 Actual 714 Projected	83 Actual 236 Projected
2011	196 Actual 740 Projected	92 Actual 244 Projected
2010	248 Actual 565 Projected	117 Actual 187 Projected
2009	271 Actual 565 Projected	146 Actual 137 Projected
2008	201 Actual 284 Projected	148 Actual 166 Projected

Not so bad in 2008, but huge misses in 2009 for single family. Multifamily projected versus actual was very close for 2009. However, thereafter both single and multifamily variances from actual versus projected was large. We believe this is due to the community's inability to build the waterfront project. The city voted not to provide economic incentives for the recreational and open-space components of the development, causing investors and lenders to look at other developments around the county where live, work and play concepts have been brought together in great development sites.

Office Demand

Office demand can be quickly calculated by taking employment numbers and dividing it by the total occupied office square feet in a market. In the following example, if the total employed is 125,212 people and the occupied office space is 87,880 people resulting in 0.7 square feet per employee. This 0.7 can then be multiplied to the projected employment growth in a community, resulting in positive, or even negative, direct annual absorption (increases or decreases in the occupied office space).

Office Market Absorption Projections

	Current Statistics								
	(A) MSA Non-Agricultural Wage & Salary Employment					25,380			
	(B) 2nd Quarter 2008 Office Inventory					103,388			
	(C) 2nd Quarter 2008 Occupied Office Space (overall)					87,880	85.0%		
	Leased Space/Total Employment (2008)					3.5			

Year		Total Employed	Employment Growth %	Annual Workers Added	Office Inventory	Occupied Office Space	SF/ Employee	Direct Annual Absorption (SF)	Direct Available	Annual Supply Change
Actual										
Year-end	2008	125,212	0.27%	335	103,388	87,880	0.7	0	15.0%	N/A
Projected										
Year-end	2009	125,547	-0.62%	335	103,388	88,115	0.7	235	14.8%	0
Year-end	2010	124,765	0.85%	(783)	103,388	87,566	0.7	(549)	15.3%	0
Year-end	2011	125,822	2.10%	1,057	103,388	88,308	0.7	742	14.6%	0
Year-end	2012	128,466	2.05%	2,644	103,388	90,164	0.7	1,856	12.8%	0
Year-end	2013	131,101	2.05%	2,635	103,388	92,013	0.7	1,849	11.0%	0
5 Year Average			1.29%	1,178			0.7	827	13.7%	0
5 Year Total			6.43%	5,889				4,133		0

Notes: Projections for employment growth based on local economists projections.

Given today's technologies, do firms really need as much office space as they did in 2008 to 2013? Laptop computers and tablets are the norm, and the tools provided to employees can allow them to conduct work virtually anywhere there is a WiFi signal. So while this example showed that 5,889 workers added to the community will result in the need for only 4,133 square feet of office space and a 13.7% direct available vacancy for the entire market, disruptive technologies have virtually stopped new construction of office space in this community. While growth in traditional office space may not be feasible, shared and collaborative workspaces (like what Starbucks did for coffee drinkers who brought their computers to socialize and work) would bring people out of their homes and help create not only a sense of community, but also shared ideas on how to solve business problems.

Open Space

Central Park in New York is the pinnacle of successful open space deployment. There are early morning joggers and bikers passing yoga, Tai Chi and meditation groups who flourish in the middle of a chaos of honking cabs and mothers yelling at their children not to run into the crosswalk. In the 1990's, the demand for housing proximity to open space created lot price premiums (price above the average lot price) as high and even more that lots with golf course frontages. Lot price premiums of $100,000 or more for oceanfront lots can be found along Mexico's oceanfront resort markets, while the price of a lot can be 25% to 50% less one street back, and another 25% to 50% less two and three streets back from the ocean.

When marketing a new master planned development, the developer's sales team establishes lot price premiums. An example is the Eldorado golf course community in Cabo San Lucas, Mexico. A developer purchased the land and 18-hole golf course, repositioned golf holes fronting the oceanfront with estate home lots and condominiums, substantially enhancing the economics of the development. Moving two holes inland provided new oceanfront real estate inventory and created enough sales revenue to substantially reduce the cost basis in the acquisition. The lots and condominiums within this community are now priced at some of the highest levels in all of Mexico.

Before an investor makes an acquisition, they need to evaluate regional and local listing and sale prices, and then take that data to determine variations in pricing relative to each property's street frontage, views and proximity to open space. The conclusions from this analysis can help investors find possible anomalies in area list prices in order to purchase real estate at below market levels. And knowing what an area's base price and premiums for frontage on or proximity to open space is a key indicator in successfully purchasing real estate at a discount.

Baby Boomer Demand

Retirement Market Fundamentals

As the U.S. population ages, the characteristics of the nation's retirement market continues to change and evolve. Today's retirees are younger, healthier, and wealthier than ever before, and their preferences for a retirement lifestyle are becoming more sophisticated. It is estimated that only 4.5% of Americans age 65 and older move during any given year. Yet, while the vast majority of retirees plan to "age in place," that is, stay in their existing homes and neighborhoods after retirement, many plan to retire to a new location. Some will even purchase a second home. These "mobile" retirees tend to be healthier and more affluent than their "stay at home" counterparts.

According to *Housing America's Seniors*, a report released by the Joint Center for Housing Studies at Harvard University, roughly 10%

of each state's population will be over the age of 65 by the year 2025. Not surprisingly, the vast majority of retirees own their own home. There are nearly 21 million active adult homeowners age 55 to 74 in the U.S.

In general, the most popular retirement destinations tend to be small towns and cities as opposed to large metropolitan areas. These smaller markets – often second, third, and fourth tier markets – offer retirees a slower pace of life and a stronger sense of community. Of the 50 to 59 age group:

- 48% indicated they will move to another state upon retirement;

- 53% of those moving to another state say a higher cost of living would deter them from moving to a different state;

- 70% of those who will move cite more affordable housing as their most important reason for moving;

- 66% of those who will move indicate they seek a better community lifestyle;

- 26% of those who will move for retirement would definitely consider an active adult community;

- 94% want 2 or more bedrooms; and

- The most desirable housing feature is wiring for the internet.

There are notable differences between the second-home buyers versus the retirement-home buyers. But two common characteristic is that a majority of both desire water access and/or views of something other than their neighbor's house. While pre-retirees made up a large investment market in pre-2007 that has largely disappeared. Baby boomers will continue to position their investments prior to retiring in order to positively affect their long term quality of life.

Some U.S. communities have a unique opportunity to position for sale and rental housing oriented toward retirees. This is the largest segment of demand for homes and rentals. Properties with open space (parks, wildlife areas, hiking and biking trails), water frontage, proximity to downtown, quick access to hospital facilities, and overall low cost all bode well for a successful age restricted, active community lifestyle development opportunity. Using big data to evaluate the trends of baby boomers is the key to successfully attracting them to any real estate community and development.

Retail Market Analysis

Small communities with populations of approximately 80,000 can have significantly larger trade areas of almost 300,000 that cross state boundaries due to even more rural areas feeding retail demand. Most of the local area's retail inventory is typically located along well-traveled highways or arterials, with retail strip centers (un-anchored retail), big box stores (large retailers in large buildings), chain restaurants (fast food and dine in), as well as a regional mall. However, this space competes with secondary retail strip centers and freestanding commercial buildings (dentist, insurance agent, convenience store) situated closer to subdivisions and housing. Typically, a community's zoning and master planned ordinances (zoning is a police power enacted by the government) will designate additional commercial land for future development. The following is an example of the calculated square foot of retail space per person in a community that can be used as the basis in making future demand projections:

	Retail Space	Population	Retail Space per Person
Retail Space Without Malls	206,642	84,238	**2.45**
Retail Space With Malls	1,559,642	80,268	**19.43**

It is evident that the mall has a significant impact on the retail space demand in the community. With only 2.45 square feet of retail space per person without including the mall area, the increase to 19.43 square feet of retail space per person when you include the mall area; that is substantial. Going forward, this community has a significant reliance on the economic impact of the mall. But given changing buyer habits and retailers providing online-internet order systems, there are some malls around the U.S. who are falling into the Dead Malls of America list (www.deadmalls.com). And repurposing a regional mall is no small task. The adverse effects to the mall owner, lender and even the community are intense. The trickle down to homeowners in the area, and even the small home rental investor, is real. Therefore, it is more important than ever for investors, lenders, retailers and even small communities to embrace big data collection and analysis. Knowing the changing retail buying trends of a community can help all players manage change.

Investors need to know not only what is currently built, but also what is under construction and planned construction. The analysis discussed here allows investors to evaluate the feasibility of new inventory. During periods of construction, there is typically a period of increased vacancy that tends to get absorbed when new additions to a market cease. However, investors of a tendency to 'pile on' numerous new construction projects in large metropolitan areas when vacancy is tight and rents are increasing. Too much construction tends to affect Class A and B assets, more so than C and D assets. As an investor, positioning the type of assets you own in a cyclical market is important to long term success.

SMALL BUSINESS CAN IMPLEMENT BIG DATA IN THEIR BUSINESS

Big data as a broad concept can be overwhelming when considering how it can impact your real estate niche as well as how you can implement its benefits into your business. Many think that the concept is too complex or expensive. Navigating through the intricacies of how it can be implemented into a business is daunting. The Big Data phenomenon resembles that of outsourcing in the first decade of the new millennium. Thomas Friedman's The World Is Flat provided clear examples of how the single person photography business, all the way to the publicly traded heavyweight, could take advantage of the ability to partner with entities or citizens in foreign countries using technology. In this same way, big data is being used by savvy businesses in real estate and beyond to increase productivity and acquire business intelligence.

As a residential appraisal firm, there is a very tricky industry landscape to navigate. With the emergence of increased regulation by way of Dodd Frank Wall Street Reform and Consumer Protection Act, the Appraisal Foundation, and the Appraisal Qualifications Boards, the federal and state governments have created a poor climate to attract and retain licensed appraisers. To become an appraiser, an applicant must have a college degree, take hundreds of hours of specified appraisal education, and find a mentor who will hold their hand during the first 2 years as an appraisal trainee.

This increased barrier to entry along with the more demanding scrutiny placed upon appraisers by government sponsored entities, state regulatory boards, and appraiser's clients through Dodd Frank, have created an exodus of appraisers with almost no appraisers entering the business. In fact, prior to the subprime mortgage crisis, there were about 105,000 appraisers in the U.S. Today, the appraisal population stands at about 76,075 and is expected to decrease at similar rates per year for the foreseeable future according to the Appraisal Institute's "US Valuation Profession Fact Sheet - June 2016".

This decline in the appraiser population is in no way related to the amount of demand for appraisals. Appraisal demand has remained constant from 2011 to 2016 given the low interest rate environment. The Appraiser Management Company (AMC) model has intentionally or otherwise set out to replace the midsized firm and encourage appraisers to work from their homes on their own with little need for peer interaction. This caused price cuts for appraisals versus cost plus fee increases as appraisers have additional oversight and regulatory requirements.

This is accomplished by most AMCs adopting a haircut model of appraiser pricing. The lender and customer of the AMC agrees to pay the standard fee for appraisals and leaves it to the AMC to negotiate with the independent fee appraiser to provide the actual assignment. The AMC takes its fee from the fixed price agreed upon with the lender and the appraiser is left with the net revenue; often a discount of 20-40% of the fee if contracted directly between the lender and the appraiser. There is a move recently to encourage AMCs to negotiate the lender fee on a cost-plus basis; meaning that the AMC fee is an add-on to the appraisal fee. While well intentioned, it is not a common practice in many AMCs.

AMCs control the clear majority of appraisal order volume. Mid-size appraisal firms typically split the fee with the staff appraiser. The Haircut AMC model puts the mid-sized appraisal firm at a distinct disadvantage to solo appraisers working out of their bedrooms. Solo appraisers with little overhead could accept assignments for less than their mid-sized counterparts since they were keeping the entire fee. Mid-sized appraisal firms have a difficult time creating compensation plans to attract appraisers with a fee split compensation model. The mid-sized firm was the market segment that was taking the time to recruit, train, and educate new appraisers in the marketplace. *With their role severely diminished and the increased barriers to entry, mid-sized firms have the compounding effect of few appraisers to train or hire.*

In this chapter, a case study is presented in which Big Data concepts along with outsourcing have been applied to a residential appraisal business to increase revenues by 500% along with the processes implemented to manage the increased volume and daily workflow. The path to determining where large amounts of data can be implemented for efficiencies is a multi-step process that may require you to look at your business in ways you haven't before.

The first step is to assess your business: identify the availability of data, the business and industry realities, and learn what existing technology providers in the market have to offer.   The appraisal business is data intensive with sources that are commonly used being county appraisal district (CAD) records for individual properties, Multiple Listings Service (MLS) for sales data, as well as other sources like flood maps and census tract. Each of these sources is available "in the cloud," or in other words, they are viewable and available online.   Thanks to the Public Records Act, bulk CAD records can be purchased inexpensively (usually less than $200) directly from the county as a single excel or CSV file. MLS data is available to be downloaded with common subscriptions when used for appraisal purposes.   The availability of these data sources is a key component to being able to access and aggregate it.

Next, the appraisal business is form or report centric. On any given standard full appraisal (FNMA Form 1004), there are over 1,000 fields that must be filled out to complete an appraisal report. The residential appraisal business is fractured with the average firm size being approximately 1 to 1.5 people. In this common "one person shop" model, each appraiser has almost no administrative support for compiling the information needed to populate those 1,000 fields of data for each report. Thus, appraisal report completion is incredibly inefficient with little technological development over the last 20 years aside from the digital camera to assist the appraiser.   Existing software applications used by appraisers to write appraisal reports are computer programs downloaded to each appraiser's computer and not in the cloud. The major software providers have a strong hold on market share with large expense budgets and they have little motivation to revolutionize the industry with new technology.

With those 1,000 fields come decisions required to determine how each field should be populated. In a 2014 article entitled "Appraisers ONLY must make 700 plus decisions in the Next Six Hours" WorkingRE magazine reporter, Diana Jacobs clearly identifies that the complexity of a traditional appraisal that requires about 700 decisions to fill out those 1,000 fields.   That's a lot of decisions to produce a low-margin, time-intensive report! The astute analysts, however, will not stop there. It is important to follow this up with further questions. Of those 700 decisions, how many must be made by the appraiser himself? Can some decisions be made by an assistant? Does that assistant have to work in the same office? Can some decisions not made by the appraiser be done by someone with little formal training or no license? If so, then how many? Can the appraiser provide input or direction at the outset that will guide the formally or informally trained assistant into an appropriate decision for any given report? If an appraiser makes a set of decisions, can proper population of additional fields be deduced by an assistant or computer algorithm? And, of course, can any of those decisions be automated by a programmed decision tree based on a set of known parameters about a market or subject property or based on an appraiser's initial molding of the assignment? These questions highlight the importance of no longer accepting the status quo of tackling one field or one decision at a time in a manual way.

On another front, managing appraisal assignments from an administrative perspective has become increasingly burdensome. The residential appraisal business was commoditized in the mid 1980's, and ever since, many mortgage appraisers find themselves competing on price and speed. Over the last 15 years and through the nudging of Dodd Frank, AMC's have taken over appraisal ordering and management from large banks. These AMC's have become the main clients of mortgage appraisers. The AMC is judged by their clients, the big banks, mainly on production metrics tied to profit margin and timing. Appraisers are often required to issue daily update requests on all open orders. In addition, appraisal reports are met with extra scrutiny once delivered to the client and revision requests or stipulations require appraisers to revisit the report and redeliver it multiple times. The administrative burden has increased significantly the need for real time process flow monitoring as part of the daily business.

This previously-mentioned extra scrutiny comes in many ways, but one of the examples is FNMA's Collateral Underwriter Database. The Collateral Underwriter endeavor by FNMA is a great example of an entity setting itself up to take advantage of big data. FNMA receives millions of appraisals per year to value collateral on loans they purchase and pool. For decades, FNMA was doing little with those millions of appraisals and the data within them. The subprime mortgage crisis highlighted the need for the government sponsored entities to take better advantage of available technologies and the wealth of data coming by way of the millions of appraisals every year. FNMA set about a multi-year plan to first standardize the fields within a standard residential appraisal to ensure that all appraisers across the country were using standardized language when describing a subject property or comparable sales and that data could then easily be separated from the form template that appraisal clients were familiar with.

Through MISMO XML data standards, FNMA created the relative language for all appraisers to use when describing unique features of a home-like quality, condition, location, view, days on market, contract date, sold date, etc. and required that appraisers (through appraisal report writers) deliver, along with PDF's of their appraisal report, a XML file containing only the data and field tags, thereby separating the data from the form. The Collateral Underwriter (CU) database now has millions of appraisals, an equal number of complete data sets on subject properties, and likely hundreds of millions of sales comparables. The database keeps track of every time a sale comes into the database, which appraiser put forth the data, and what data was used. FNMA requires every lender to run each appraisal, once signed and delivered, through CU for a data consistency and reasonability check against the data warehouse. The data, along with risk algorithms, assigns a risk score in seconds to the appraisal on a scale from 1-5, with which the lender can make the decision on whether to proceed with the loan or not.

FNMA knows how the appraiser has used every sale on every report as well as how the appraiser's peers have used that same sale. Over the last several years, the industry is ripe with stories of appraisers receiving letters from FNMA pointing out inconsistencies in how appraisers used the same comparable sales in multiple reports. As you can imagine, this brings on a whole new level of scrutiny for the appraiser. Some appraisers have had their license revoked as a consequence. While tough for the appraiser, the public and private FNMA is following through on ensuring the public trust in home lending by making sure to use all tools at their disposal to regulate and maintain integrity within the appraiser business. ***But these tools and this database are not made available to the appraisers who are creating it.*** The appraiser's liability is set in stone once they sign the report and before they know how the CU will judge their work.

The government sponsored entities (GSEs) are using big data to review and critique the appraisers. Given the commodity nature of the business, competition based on speed and price, dwindling supply of licensed appraisers available in the market, lack of a good way to check his work versus his peers BEFORE signing a report and delivering it to a client/FNMA's CU, the individual independent fee appraiser is literally under attack. The lack of technological development to speed up report writing and the increasing administrative burden in managing a volume appraisal business has hurt both the sole practitioner, as well as the appraisal firm.

What to Do Now?

We have described an industry with little industry-wide technological development amidst significant change from many directions including major big data applications. All the players except the appraiser are large, mostly national firms. Appraisers and appraisal firms must find a way to compete, including the use of big data tools. ***However, it is vital to understand that implementation of big data on its own will seldom be effective.*** New process creation is a pivotal component that is equally important to making use of big data.

Our analysis of the market indicates big data is needed but several steps are required to achieve it:

1. Identify the availability of needed data sources in the cloud that make aggregation and automation possible.

2. Given the small firm size and fractured nature of the industry, investment required to develop big data applications is likely beyond most firm's capacities. An alternative path is needed to pioneer a new system using current cloud based technology and cloud based support software.

3. Creation of alternative automation, or assignment to assistants a portion of the labor-intensive form filling process.

4. If volume can be created, a trainee business model allowing trainees to begin assisting on less critical interim decisions until ready to move to more critical, appraiser-guided decisions.

5. Compartmentalize the data gathering, report writing, and analysis process sufficient to provide acceptable income to trainee, appraiser, and firm.

6. In a growth mindset, and with limited appraisers available to hire to complete the work, an opportunity to make the firm appraisers more efficient is needed, thereby increasing their billings.

7. The need to automate an assignment log (also called order management system, the company's application to monitor assignment performance and progress to completion) to seamlessly produce business intelligence for internal analysis and communication outputs to be communicated efficiently with clients.

8. The need for appraisers to have access to a data warehouse containing an appraiser's data as well as his peers' data, like FNMA's Collateral Underwriter, to analyze the report BEFORE signing it, which creates the "no turning back" professional liability.

We systemically researched and studied each of these points.

1. The availability of needed data sources in the cloud make aggregation and automation possible

Seeing that data was both available in the cloud and available in bulk for purchase for minimal cost, we acquired the data in the counties that our firm covers. This data entailed millions of properties and included both residential and commercial records. Commercial records could be saved for later, since the firm's focus is on residential. Each record has approximately 70 fields of data. This data was loaded into a virtual database hosted in Rackspace to establish a base record for every parcel in 16 counties. Included in the database are fields of data that can populate roughly 150 of the 1,000 fields of input in standard form appraisal report.

The next step, and most commonly used data in our business, is MLS information. MLS information is a very well protected dataset, as its data is considered by the MLS as very valuable. As subscribers to each MLS, we can download MLS sales relevant to each individual analysis. All MLS data is available in the cloud and comes with easy to export tools right on the MLS websites. In our practice, this MLS data is processed and downloaded at the beginning of the appraisal assignment so that it can be matched with county tax rolls in our database, and then is ready for analysis and population into our form appraisal report. With this MLS data, roughly 35% of the 1,000 fields of data can be inputted in an automated way. Not only can the data be inputted, but also simple algorithms were written to make sure that the data interpreted from both MLS and CAD populates the government forms in the specific way that the FNMA requires. This automation removes all chance of typos and miscommunication.

In our business, we have the resources to even take the data a step further. A team of trained researchers review each MLS sale individually and decipher or assign a quality, condition, location, and view ranking. This assists the appraiser in running regression and other analytics on the set of data in ways that are presently unavailable on the market. More on that later.

With the data available in a cloud database, the appraiser can use a variety of software applications to derive an output of his choosing. The data can be exported into excel, xml, or any other format required for use. In our case, several of the software companies who have appraisal report writing software have "stores" that allow third party products "back door access" to populating the forms. Additionally, some of the fields have Excel applications built within that software to accept a string of data and populate the form in a useful way.

With the data in the cloud and our most commonly used data sources aggregated, our firm is set up to have data efficiently accessible and useable to our team. Additionally, we have found fields of data that neither data source provides. We have taken steps to manually create inputs for the fields (quality, condition, location, and view) as it would be useful to our team. At the outset, we created this data manually, but there are options to begin to automate. More on that later.

2. **Given the small firm and fractured nature of the industry, a special entrepreneur is needed to pioneer a new, better way using current cloud based technology and new cloud based applications.**

As previously noted, there are ways to take our cloud database we have created and get it into existing software applications, but they all require extra steps. Extra steps in our low margin, commodity business is a productivity drag and is also an obstacle to getting folks to implement change or make use of the data. Existing appraisal report writing options cannot take advantage of modern technology as they are programs that reside on each user's personal computer or server. Instead, these applications must be in the cloud so seamless communication between application and database can take place.

Our firm is fortunate to have access to a wealth of programming resources and capitalized sufficiently to take on the task of being a pioneer of a new cloud based appraisal report writer. It has been clear that the appraisal industry has needed change but simply didn't have the motivation from the major stakeholders to make it happen. Our firm believed that if we could build a cloud based application with website access connected to the database that we built, appraisers outside of our firm would find it useful, and be willing to adapt our process for the efficiencies and improvement in quality of their appraisal reports that the system would provide.

We set out to build an appraisal report writer that, at the time of this writing, is being beta tested internally in our firm. The application is accessible through a website, and our entire team uses this system to complete appraisal reports. The application accesses the national database and can perform seamless two-way communication between the user interface and the database. If the appraiser makes a change to the size of the house or the year built, the database can immediately take that data and add it as a data point to the record. On the next assignment where that property is used, the appraiser can see that they made the change to that record. The appraisal data has immediately been improved with no additional work by the appraiser. *What if I shared that data with the rest of the appraisers in our firm? What if we agreed to share this data with all our peers in the market? It could be a game changer!*

Going through the exercise of creating our own internal cloud application has allowed us to examine current technologies and improve upon that which modern technology allows. In addition to the application being able to connect to cloud based data sources, the user interface has completely changed. Gone are the days of the 30-50 page appraisal for which you can scroll each appraiser has memorized. In its place is a progress bar, a logical order of operations, of decisions, and a system that is easily followed by any novice user introduced to the platform. Training becomes easier and the appraisal process can be better understood by the support staff.

Furthermore, FNMA has been encouraging appraisers over the last several years to support adjustments applied in the sales comparison grid by analysis such as regression or paired sales analysis. Many companies offer such a service, but their application leaves a bit to be desired given the appraiser's profit motive. Whether regression analysis is included in a report or not, the appraiser is getting the same fee and most often not losing clients if the data isn't present. Having an ancillary application that they must log into, export data from MLS, import into the application, then spends 20-30 minutes refining and analyzing that data is a proposition that many in the industry understandably reject. However, with our cloud based report writing application connected to all the data the appraiser will need, regression analysis can be run in the background automatically as soon as the appraiser chooses the subject property and defines the market area using polygon mapping tools which are necessary to begin an appraisal analysis. So, in the background, regression is being run so that it is ready to present to the user at the time he needs it, when applying adjustments.

In creating this application, we are only scratching the surface for what's possible, as all previous obstacles have been overcome by embracing modern technology: new software, available data bases, cloud software, and big data.

3. To automate or assign to assistants a portion of the labor-intensive form filling process

We developed a database containing the necessary data sources. Senior management then went through the process of developing a web application to create a data pipeline funnel and report system. We then connected the data sources to the report system all the way to each step of the assignment, completing the appraisal, to receiving final payment.

This detailed analysis was intensive. We held a magnifying glass to everything we did from an administrative perspective as well as a professional perspective. It required us to challenge industry norms of "what has to be done by an appraiser" until we arrived at a genuine analysis of what was clerical or basic data gathering, and what required the professional skills of the appraiser. These activities were grouped into directed tasks, appraiser-supervised tasks, and those tasks required by the appraiser. We then determined what amount of training was required for each set of activities, and finally where that activity could best be done. Some tasks required more direct supervision and interaction with the appraiser. Others could be trained with written procedures and perform at different times remotely from the main office operation by someone overseas, at a substantially cheaper hourly rate.

Over the course of our analysis, we divided up the tasks into the category of employees that were required to complete the task. This left us with 15 people in Coimbatore, India, working for our company 24 hours a day. To that group, we added an expanded administrative team and appraiser assistants stateside to help in the field as well in certain parts of the appraisal reports that didn't require the appraiser and/or couldn't be automated.

Accomplishing this allowed our appraisers to be far more efficient, complete more assignments each week, and increase the volume that our firm could accept. If we handled 30-40% of the fields in a form by automation and cloud connectivity, we could handle the same amount with additional manual support, so we found that the appraisal professional only needs to handle about 20-30% of the tasks required to complete an assignment.

It may seem revolutionary, but other professions have evolved into similar task organizations; physicians, lawyers, and accountants, all have done the same.

4. **If volume can be generated, then a trainee business model can be supported. Allowing trainees to assist on less critical decisions until ready to move to more critical, appraiser-guided decisions. Compartmentalizing the data gathering, report writing, and analysis process sufficient to allow and provide acceptable income to trainee, appraiser, and the firm.**

As discussed earlier in this chapter, the state licensing model applied to the appraisal industry is having devastating effects on the appraisal landscape. There is a need for new appraisers to enter the field. The Profession is aging, and we are losing more experienced appraisers each year. Candidates are required to complete extensive formal classroom training before they can be accepted as an appraiser trainee. The traditional independent-fee appraisal business has a difficult time adding trainees who are not able to produce income for a year or more.

Breaking down the business and appraisal process in the way that we did, to compartmentalize the process and assign many duties required to complete an appraisal report, allowed us to build in a detailed training process for new trainees. A trainee can enter our operation, spend about 2-3 weeks in full-time training, then move into to phase 1 administrative duties; logging orders, performing basic research, etc., while gaining knowledge. Trainees can then move to phase 2 which requires an increase in appraisal knowledge. The final tasks qualify the trainee and to add to their experience log the tasks required by state regulators to demonstrate activities necessary to qualify for sitting for the various licensing exams. *Our business can now support training the next generation of appraisers profitably.*

5. **Compartmentalize the data gathering, report writing, and analysis process sufficient to provide acceptable income to trainee, appraiser, and firm.**

Teams are established to handle a portion of the overall tasks at hand. Data is gathered and processed by data analysts. Then the data is processed by the report writing application to pre-fill as many data fields as possible. The trainee can then add or correct any data that is missing or not exactly relative to the property, client and lender. This allows the trainee to learn the process of not only the appraisal, but also the mortgage process and players. The seasoned appraiser now employs the "science" part of the process, but at much greater speeds than ever before. Matched pair sets of the same homes sold in the market, but one may have a pool and the other not, allows the appraisers to support adjustments between the sales comparables and the subject. This can be done for two versus three car garages, fireplaces, etc. Regression analysis reviews hundreds and even thousands of homes to provide further support of adjustments. The appraiser uses this support to adjust the sale comparables to the subject. The resulting conclusion is the market value, which many times does not equal price, but in most cases is the basis for the loan. The company now provides the fastest turnaround, with the best quality analysis in the business and each participant in the process makes more money per hour than ever before.

6. **In a growth mindset, and with limited appraisers available to hire to complete the work, an opportunity exists to make the firm appraisers more efficient, and increase their billings.**

Growing a residential appraisal firm is akin to swimming upstream. The current working against us in this case is the fractured industry, dealing with heavy regulatory oversight, and a significant percentage of appraisers leaving the business. With so many appraisers leaving the industry and many others working in a small firm, between 1 to 1.5 people on average, finding the labor to complete any additional volume is challenging.

The motivating factor for our appraisal firm to explore incorporating big data was the competition. We realized we had to take significant steps to improving the firm's compensation plan for appraisers to encourage the few people looking for positions an opportunity comparable to what they could make working on their own. Additionally, their quality of life must significantly improve, as they spend far less time with the monotony of data entry and manual inputs that now don't necessarily require their time. Finally, the effect for the company was to increase volume by increasing each appraiser's capacity in a world where there is a limited supply of appraisers.

The plan worked! By focusing on dollars earned per hour, our appraisers earned twice as much while being able to compensate the assistants at a reasonable rate. This was accomplished by retaining the company gross profit margin at 47% instead of the standard 50%. With this compensation plan comes experienced and supervised trainee's earning their way to state certification. Those trainees are now nearing a point in time where they can hit the ground running and take their turn being the appraiser.

7. **The need to automate, organize, and standardize our internal order management, to seamlessly produce business intelligence for internal analysis, and to communicate efficiently with clients.**

Going from 20-30 orders per week to 80-100 orders per week alone creates a tremendous burden on the administrative department. This is especially true when you consider the increasing burden the industry is putting on appraisers from an administrative perspective. Increased communication required by each client before, during, and even after the appraisal is delivered is commonplace. Constant updates on the status of each assignment while in process is a time intensive task that requires communication between our appraisers and administration who then relay the constant updates among the 50+ client web portals.

When we began this project, our communication was not standardized. A loose exchange of emails, text messages, instant messages, phone calls, and client portal updates left the firm with the least efficient modes of communication. In many businesses, including ours, most communications happen in loose, unstructured mediums like the ones described above. Unstructured data, including report status, details about the assignment, who worked on the assignment, etc. leaves the company in a tenuous place. To quickly access the status of an assignment when a client calls on the phone was impossible. Scanning through emails and attempting to decipher the specific language the appraiser chose in describing the status takes time, and must be redone every time the information is sought. Analyzing company trends to identify issues needing resolution or identify items slowing down the delivery of assignments was impossible. Detailed billing reports could only be produced by extensive manual effort every time the report was run. Additionally, communication with our team in India required manual email communication providing instructions each day. This left much room for error and miscommunication. The fractured communications presented obstacles to quick access to both business intelligence and status of files in our system.

The missing key in our approach at the onset was the standardization of as much of the information and communication as possible. Next, it was needed in a central location so that key metrics or notes could be pulled out for analysis immediately. Again, we broke down this aspect of our business in areas such as the most commonly used status messages, stages of each assignment, major issues, and useful notes about each property. Once developed, we implemented an order management system (OMS) that monitored the appraisal process and allowed management to properly manage more assignments.

The OMS was put in the cloud so the appraiser and administration could reach the file via tablet, cell phone, or computer wherever they were, including in the field. Little to no communication was to be conducted via the unformatted mediums of email, instant message, text, etc. All communication was to be directed through the order management system. Each time a button was clicked or a box checked, a time stamp with the user who inputted it was logged. We could then tract when a file moved from one status to another, how long it stayed there, and who moved it out. Clients could easily be updated when calling ahead of time each day, now that order status was collected in a central place with common, easy to understand statuses. Additionally, reports could quickly be run to identify problem areas or slowdowns in the appraisal process. For example, was it taking an especially long time to get reports into the next status/stage after an inspection was completed? Was our internal review process taking longer than the allowed time? Was one appraiser particularly inefficient during a particular stage? All of these questions could be answered quickly with simple reporting. In addition to process analysis, financial analysis could take place much faster as well.

To complete the big data picture, we are in the process of connecting our OMS to our national database where we can easily pull in relevant subject property details, as well as link the same address from the order form to the actual appraiser in our cloud based software.

The standardization of our internal communication is a smaller but necessary application of big data in the sense that you are finding ways to capture common occurrences in your business in a way that can be analyzed on a larger level.

By breaking down and standardizing our processes, communication became simpler within our office and our executive team could efficiently manage and identify problem areas.

8. **The need for appraisers to have access to a data warehouse containing an appraiser's data as well as his peers' data, like FNMA's collateral underwriter, to analyze the report BEFORE signing it, which creates the "no turning back" professional liability.**

Much like FNMA's realization that they should standardize and make use of the wealth of data they receive every day to assess loan risk in an automated fashion, appraisers have realized they too should standardize and make use of the wealth of data that the 70,000+ appraisers are creating and delivering to clients every day. Given the fractured nature of the appraisal industry and little motivation from the leading software providers to accumulate this data for the sake of the industry and appraiser protection, the platform did not exist to warehouse this data and make it available to appraisers.

The creation of the cloud appraisal report writer that our appraisal firm has created is the software application and platform required to satisfy this industry need.

While still in the final stages of development, this platform has the capability of seamlessly collecting any appraiser-inputted field of data and storing it in the appraiser's cloud database right where the appraiser does the analysis. Because it is in the cloud, the database can then show the appraiser how they used the data in prior reports and how their peers (who use the same appraisal report writer) used data in prior reports. With the information being provided to appraisers *BEFORE* the report is signed, the appraiser avoids the exposure to the liability of losing their license or being reprimanded for using comparable data inconsistently. The same process can be presented to appraisers to assess how their sales comparison adjustments relate to what peers in that same market area have done.

In addition to the data warehouse, large clients with heavy underwriting requirements can provide the platform their specific requirements which can then be applied to the assignment *while* the analysis and report is being generated, BEFORE the signing and delivery of the original report. This can save countless hours of headache to appraisers and clients while speeding up the time to close.

In Conclusion

With the concerted effort outlined above over the course of 18-24 months, our appraisal firm has gotten into big data and used it to thrive in a very competitive environment. The productivity improvement has strengthened our firm. Our appraisers are enjoying higher incomes and increased quality of life. Independent Fee Appraisers who choose to use our cloud report writer software will receive many of the advantages our firm enjoys.

In addition, our firm's core focus is shifting. Our firm is still in the business of delivering quality appraisal reports, but big data is now a central focus. While not a goal at the outset, the software application we developed is collecting extremely valuable information that businesses around the world are missing and desperately need. Automated valuation models work to value millions of properties a day. But those models are doing the best they can without four key components that effect value in residential real estate: *quality, condition, location, and view*. With these key pieces of data now being inputted, first by our team of researchers overseas, and then verified by appraisers visiting the properties, we are accumulating an extremely valuable database that can truly improve the quality of automated valuation models. This improvement can be felt all the way up the chain of users tracking values of the assets (houses) in Residential Mortgage Backed Securities (RMBS) on Wall Street or in other bond types. Inaccurate valuations combined with underwriting exuberance resulted in the Great Recession of 2008. With improved quality, condition, location, and view data, maybe future great recessions driven by inflated collateral analysis can be avoided.

Our effort to improve our appraisal business and the businesses of other Independent Fee Appraisers has been achieved. The *Big Data in the Cloud* application has opened other lucrative business opportunities for our firm beyond the core business, opportunities which may prove to be even more profitable in the long run.

WHAT'S IN STORE FOR WALL STREET

Wall Street has always had the brightest minds playing with the best toys. Rooms of MBAs work exhaustive hours analyzing up to six computer screens delivering data from around the globe. The financial industry currently makes up about seven percent of the U.S. gross domestic product (GDP), up from a little over three percent in the 1950's. But with best in class information, advanced technologies and databases, why has the industry been so slow to adapt and create new technologies surrounding big data?

The physical banking environment is transforming into a digital and esign cloud world driven by not only consumers, but new business start-ups with technology geeks at the helm. Their disruption to the status norms is occurring now. Big institutional firms who "black boxed" (bought or created a business platform that they only use within their own company) applications have been able to increase market share. But the technology explosion of new ideas, rules-based platforms and data processing tools is coming from individuals and small, start-up companies by the thousands. This is taking the stodgy old executives by amazement and those firms that do not get on the bandwagon will lose market share or head towards Chapter 7; death by a thousand cuts.

How Data and Analytics Will Be Used in Mortgage Banking

Big data is being used for predictive analytics, like who is likely to purchase a first home, who will purchase a larger home, how much equity in one's home is needed before they refinance or apply for a home equity loan, and at what age is best to promote a reverse mortgage. On the servicing side, it will be used to address mortgage delinquencies in real time (days instead of months), tailor the mortgage default to the type of person, quickly evaluate whether the homeowner has equity, and determine if the homeowner has abandoned the home.

Some of these claims may sound like science fiction. Those of you who are 50 or older will remember the detective Dick Tracy and his watch that doubled as a phone. While we do not have flying cars or jetpacks to take us to work (yet), we do have Apple watches that serve as a phone with a data source that is amazing.

There are tens of thousands emerging businesses and those early stage start-ups that can reach maturity could bring disruptive technology, technology that changes an industry. Successful start-ups begin with low subscriber base, but quickly increase to industry norms, until a significant portion of the industry uses the information or service as their everyday tools. Since 2004, the average lifespan of a company on the S&P 500 is 20 years or less. The financing that brought those companies to life is looking for a long-term, safe and reliable payback. Wide swings in cash flow and budget expectations are frowned upon, while steady, sustainable growth is met with higher than normal stock pricing. This growth creates security for the underlying debt.

Mobile distribution allows products from companies of all sizes, including start-ups, to reach consumers quickly. And this is particularly important to millennials, who view their banking relationship as transactional, versus baby boomers, who have stayed with the banker for decades and relied on them for not only checking and savings accounts, but also for loans and investment advice. National banks and credit card companies have been on the negative side of the news for over a decade and the media's portrayal of greed has spurred groups on, like Occupy Wall Street. Millennials notice this social rebuke and applaud the willingness to push back against the wealthiest people on earth.

The 20- and 30-year olds feel no commitment to stick with one bank and are bombarded with opportunities from not only local companies, but can evaluate opportunities from around the world. And for many companies, real estate plays a significant value component in the overall company's market capitalization. Some product companies require significant distribution channels, like Budweiser, Coca-Cola and Starbucks. And let's look at retailers who need strategic corner locations to be successful, like Walgreens and CVS pharmacies. The underlying value in the real estate can be enhanced with long-term lease agreements and corporate guarantees, essentially allowing these types of businesses to use the sale-leaseback strategy to raise money. For example, a retailer buys vacant land on a high-traffic corner location for $1,000,000 ($10.00 per square foot). Then builds a building for $3,000,000 ($80.00 per square foot), for a total of $4,000,000 investment into the new retail store. The retailer sets up a lease rate based on a percentage of retail sales; say $200 per square foot in sales for the 37,500 square foot building will allow the retail to pay 8.0%, or $600,000 per year in rental rate under triple net lease terms (tenant pays all expenses in addition to the lease payment). But the retailer already knows that triple-net leased buildings in this market sell for 6.0% capitalization rates. So the retailer sells the building for $10,000,000 ($600,000 divided by 6.0%) and uses the $6,000,000 profit ($10,000,000 less $4,000,000) to fund future business operations and growth. This sale-leaseback strategy has been employed by some of the most successful retailers in the U.S.

However, if sales are not up to par, then the tenant vacates, leaving the investor and their lender holding the asset that may not be worth even $4,000,000. The investor and lender risk is substantial and many times not correctly reflected in the capitalization rate. Dark retail buildings occur in even the highest growth communities of the world and repositioning an asset sold at a premium is no easy task. And the property owners of these now defunct assets are now fighting taxing jurisdictions on using the $4,000,000 as the basis for assessed value and taxation, versus the $10,000,000 recent price. Those successful retailers that can bring the assessment down have a significant expense reduction versus those that do not.

The data needed to properly analyze investment in these triple-net assets includes land pricing, replacement and reproduction cost new, market trends on how much retail sales are, traffic volumes and trends, what percentage of revenue can retailers pay for rent, market ranges for capitalization rates, taxation trends and how 'go-dark' scenarios could affect pricing. After considering these factors, purchasing a triple-net Walgreens under a 20-year lease no longer seems like an easy analysis. Then stack up every triple-net purchase opportunity in the country and rate them by these factors, plus lease term and credit rating of the tenant, to get a prudent methodology to consider which is the best buy. This takes a tremendous amount of big data and analysis, but allows investors using big data and filters to find anomalies in the market to allow them to purchase below market.

Let's look at the life cycle of a real estate asset:

Real estate has numerous data collection points in its economic life cycle:

Owned Asset

- Rental and occupancy rates.

- Annual operating and fixed costs – maintenance, landscape, pest control, insurance, window cleaning, security, elevator, janitorial, and property taxes.

- Periodic engagements – tenant improvements, architects and engineers for new tenant space, evaluations to determine market value, and refinance opportunities.

Owner Considers Selling

- Broker price opinions and / or evaluation.

- Accountants prepare books.

Owner Engages in Sale Process

- Broker contracts for engagement, solicits prospective buyers and manages closing process;

- Third party reports ordered; environmental, appraisal, survey, federal tax statements and property inspectors.

Owner Sells Asset

- Owner becomes a seller that may be positioned for a 1031 exchange or look to purchase another real estate asset.

New Owner

- Like the prior owner, property economics, annual and fixed costs and periodic engagements all need to be re-evaluated.

There are over 1,000 data collection points in just the 1004 residential appraisal form or in narrative commercial appraisal reports. Big data focuses not only all of the data points in the process, but also collects the data on the people involved in the process: owner / seller, brokers, appraisers, engineers, leasing agents, real estate and mortgage brokers, banker / lender prospects, buyer prospects, etc. With the ability to evaluate every loan done on the real estate asset being sold in a particular market, buyers, like no time in the past, can evaluate lending options efficiently.

Let's now review the options for both mortgage originators and servicers in using big data.

Identifying Mortgage Prospects

The key to identifying mortgage prospects is to gather granular data on recent borrowers and then to identify people with similar characteristics. Some of the data may be available in your files. Other data may need to be sourced from public records or data providers.

An effective marketing and sales campaign also has to be employed. Convincing millennials to borrow money is the easy part, attracting them to your company's business platform is another story. Businesses need to employ social media initiatives and search engine optimization tools to stay at the forefront of prospective young borrowers who are about to take over the financial industry. Hundreds of start-up companies are working on technology and applications to process data quicker and make the lending process easier. The mere thought of having to read and sign hundreds of pages of loan closing documents in paper is turning off future generations of homeowners.

Refinances

As a starting point, let us ponder what causes homeowners to refinance, not refinance, or get a second mortgage. Psychographics provide data on the economic status, age, marital status and children in a house. A variety of firms have this data available including Nielsen, who segments each U.S. house. Your first step is to have a data provider classify each of your recent clients by psychographic profile. A reasonable next step would be to review factors such as prior mortgage rate versus new mortgage rate, and the loan to value ratio (loan amount divided by property value). The next step would be to identify homeowners who: 1) fit your prime psychographic profile (could be empty nesters or first time home buyers in predominantly single story small to medium home size subdivisions); and 2) have similar interest rates above current market levels, and loan to value characteristics.

Since interest rates have been low for a long time, a more interesting project is to identify homeowners with a mortgage rate differential likely to be 2% or higher, and then analyze their psychographic profile. This problem is more interesting; why would someone turn down "free money" if they could reduce the interest rate on their home loan by 2%? Based on analysis, it appears there are millions of such homeowners. Perhaps in some situations the market value has fallen or they have credit problems and can't qualify for a loan. While this accounts for some who have not refinanced, it does not account for the majority. The next reasonable step is market research in the form of phone surveys, direct mail surveys or focus groups to determine why those homeowners are paying a higher interest rate than necessary.

Second Mortgages

The reasons for second mortgages include consolidating credit card debt, vacations, home expansion or remodeling, college expenses, weddings and more. The simplest starting point is getting psychographic data on recent refinance clients and then finding homeowners who have similar psychographic profiles and have adequate equity. However, it is probably possible to further narrow the best prospects after evaluating why homeowners with specific psychographic profiles obtained second mortgages. If you find that a target psychographic profile gets second mortgages for college costs, you can then seek a data source that indicates which of these households have children about to enter college or children in college. We are just scratching the surface here. Given the data sources and analytics available, it is possible to narrow the list of targets who want a loan for a specific purpose, so the marketing can be targeted.

Mortgage Servicing

The first step a mortgage servicer should do is mine the treasure trove of information available in the loan origination file, including any allowable personal information. A second step would be to obtain psychographic data for all borrowers. The third step is to load all this information into a system that allows customer service staff to see as much information on individual borrowers, groups of borrowers and borrowers organized in other ways such as loan amount, estimated loan to value, origination date, location, occupation, and date of typical loan payment. This is the short list; a customer service representative or manager could provide many more metrics.

Remember, the three Vs of big data are volume, velocity and variety. Here we will focus on **velocity** after considering a variety of data. Do not wait until a borrower is 30 or 60 days late to send a delinquency notice. Call the borrower and send a delinquency note 3 to 5 days after the grace period. The borrower needs to know you are at the top of the list to be paid or you will be a squeaky wheel.

Assume you are able to contact the borrower and learn they are having financial difficulties. However, they have previously paid timely for ten years. Another borrower, when contacted, is late for the fifth time in 12 months. Addressing delinquencies real time and gaining insight into the basis for the problem minimizes the delinquent interest and provides data for a prudent decision. Each reason for a delinquency should be a code to allow analysis.

Many companies are adopting big data and the means to analyze their business in real time. Most companies operate on lean margins, typically less than ten percent. Big data is no longer a futuristic concept like Dick Tracy's 1960 watch-phone. Big data is being rapidly integrated into business today. Business leaders at progressive companies need to start or accelerate the adoption of big data or risk being yesterday's news.

Big Data and Loan Servicing

Big data is the latest event in the accelerating pace of human change. Humans started farming between 6,000 to 9,000 BC, or about 8,000 to 11,000 years ago. In Western history, the industrial revolution started about 1800. The information revolution became main stream in 1976 with the first Apple computer. Big data became a mainstream concept around 2010. The time from farming to the industrial revolution was about 7,000 years, to computers another 180 years and to big data only 30 years. The next step after big data will be systems to analyze the data and use it for decision making. What comes next is uncertain and unknown, but it will be here quickly.

Loan Servicing in the Good Old Days

Few in the workforce remember loan servicing before Lewis Ranieri created securitization for single family loans in 1977. Mr. Ranieri is recognized in both Liars' Poker and in the Big Short. Before he started purchasing and securitizing thousands and hundreds of thousands of home loans, the institution that originated them serviced them. They were balance sheet loans made by banks and savings and loans. Incredible in today's world, before 1977 the person who made the loan often handled problems with servicing. But there were few problems. The last bill a person would default on was typically the home mortgage.

Big Data Described

Big data has many definitions. Ours is simple: big data combines a variety of data sources that facilitate understanding, insights and decision making. Less important than having gargantuan size data tables is having a variety of well selected datasets whose confluence provides clarity in understanding complex and intractable problems. The US census is a huge dataset but does not qualify as big data. The addresses, loan amounts, and payment history for a million loans would not alone qualify as big data. However, start adding factors such as the value of collateral, loan to value, date the loan was originated, the company that originated the loan, the loan officer, and quality of loan documentation (routine or NINJA or stated income), and you can start to quickly discern patterns and start to estimate which loans are at risk.

Loan Servicing is Now Much More Complicated

There are still loans that are made and serviced by the same person. However, today these are jumbo loans for affluent borrowers who have other relationships with the bank. Securitization has created a new industry known as loan servicing. If the loan officer who made the loan is not available to speak to the borrower, who do they call? There are two factors about loan servicing that are indisputable: 1) loan servicing can be lucrative but the fees are very competitive, and 2) if a loan has been securitized, it is difficult, if not impossible, to get authority from the bond holders to modify the loan. (Once a loan is securitized, the tranches – different levels of risk such as AAA, AA, A, BBB, BB, etc – have been sold to different institutional investors who have disparate interests.)

However, those are the easy changes. Congress has passed legislation, including the Dodd Frank Act, for which the regulatory agencies still have not written enabling legislation, which are inconsistent and virtually assure that every mortgage servicer is subject to inadvertently violating the law. Just a few of the requirements of Dodd-Frank are:

- Each servicer of any federally related mortgage loan shall notify the borrower in writing of any assignment, sale, or transfer of the servicing of the loan to any other person.

- If any servicer of a federally related mortgage loan receives a qualified written request from the borrower (or an agent of the borrower) for information relating to the servicing of such loan, the servicer shall provide a written response acknowledging receipt of the correspondence within 5 days (excluding legal public holidays, Saturdays, and Sundays) unless the action requested is taken within such period.

- DAMAGES AND COSTS - Whoever fails to comply with any provision of this section shall be liable to the borrower for each such failure in the following amounts...

- CLASS ACTIONS - In the case of a class action, an amount equal to the sum of...

- Fail to respond within 10 business days to a request from a borrower to provide the identity, address, and other relevant contact information about the owner or assignee of the loan.

Lawsuits and Consent Agreements

Never mind there are no reported cases of wrongful foreclosure, the federal government has sued virtually every large bank, extracted "settlements" typically in excess of $1 billion and required them to enter into agreements more onerous than Dodd Frank. The banks that entered into settlements and consent decrees include the following: Wells Fargo, Bank of America, CitiBank, PNC Bank, EverBank, JP Morgan Chase, One West, Santander Bank, and U. S. National Bank. Loan servicer Ocwen entered into a settlement with the attorney generals in 49 states and with the federal government.

From the writer's perspective, the volume of loan defaults escalated at a rate no one expected and the loan servicers did their best to handle the defaults. The lawsuits by the federal government and attorney generals were a stalling action to delay the foreclosure activity action.

The lifecycle of loan servicing can be broken into four simple segments: 1) on-boarding, 2) routine serving, 3) preliminary default and 4) default requiring foreclosure or a workout. Each segment is examined along with thoughts on how big data can be integrated.

On-Boarding

Many loan servers handle either paper documents or scanned documents that can only be read or queried using PDF or an optical character recognition file. The first critical stage is to generate loan documents with a loan processing system that generates images as well as indexes to the images. First, this will sharply reduce the time to on-board a file. Second, it will make it possible to do validations not possible without an electronic file. Consider validation of the following issues:

- Is this the borrower's primary residence or is he also claiming multiple other first residences?

- Is the reported sales price consistent with the assessed value for property taxes?

- Verification of borrower identity using electronic contact with third party service.

- Extracting key loan and deed of trust terms to affirm they are consistent with the tape or other documentation presented.

- Confirming that all required documents, based on state law and location, have been received. For example, in Texas, a municipal utility district (MUD) document is required if the property is in a MUD. In certain coastal areas, borrowers must affirm they understand the risk of storms.

- Electronic loan processing systems can provide a list of completed documents and whether all documents have been completed.

- Are the dates in the documents consistent with the loan?

- Are there additional documents, such as a release of lien, that have been filed?

- Is the current flood determination and flood policy appropriate?

- Is the monthly property tax escrow reasonable based on the assessed value and tax rates?

- How about if the property is new construction purchased in December which will be reassessed on full value in January?

- If the loan is being on-boarded from another servicer, have all appropriate documents been produced?

All of these tasks can be done manually, but often they are not. However, all of these tasks can be performed electronically with the proper system.

Routine Servicing

During routine servicing a big data platform can minimize costs, maximize collections and likely minimize regulatory trouble. We will next review events other than monetary defaults. Lenders will seldom pursue foreclosure for a non-monetary default. However, they should be aware and be tracking such events.

Non-Monetary Defaults

Non-monetary defaults should be considered an early warning system of possible problems. Following are examples of non-monetary defaults:

- A borrower has routinely made payments 5 to 10 days prior to the first of the month. However, they now are arriving a day or two after the first of the month.

- A borrower has routinely been making monthly payments of $500 in addition to the principal, interest, taxes and insurance (PITI). However, they revert to the basic minimum payment.

- The borrower is sued by the home owner's association (HOA) for not paying HOA dues.

- An abstract of judgment is filed against a debtor.

- The borrower's mailing address, which has been the collateral for the loan, changes to another city or state.

- The local government files a lien against the collateral claiming the property to be uninhabitable.

- The borrowers, a married couple, file for divorce.

- The borrower obtains a tax loan to pay the taxes; the lender places a lien on the property.

While each of these in the abstract seems minor, they do contain useful information. When evaluated over a portfolio of 1 million or more mortgages, the implications of each can be evaluated with predictive results allowing lenders to make decisions real-time.

Monetary Defaults

Historical reports have indicated that few loan workouts have been successful. At the very least, big data can help to determine which are likely to be successful and which are not. However, early contact with the borrower to understand the circumstances and to evaluate their chance of success can be both humane and financially appropriate. Consider the following events of financial default:

- George is a gardener. He just bought a $900,000 home using a stated income loan. He missed the first payment. His stated income was $300,000. When you discuss George's income and how much he can afford for a monthly payment, he indicates between $500 and $600 per month. The best option is likely to make a deal with George to get him to move, perhaps giving him moving money, and proceeding with foreclosure.

- Ron is a skilled machinist, married for 30 years. He bought a $200,000 home five years ago and is 15 days late on his payment for the first time. He reports his prior employer closed without notice and he has 3 offers at a similar or higher wage rate. Assuming the servicer believes Ron, it would make sense to extend him every courtesy, work closely (weekly?) with him to get a payment plan that works and get him back on schedule.

- Robert is a skilled geologist in west Houston who lives in a $700,000 house. He bought the house 12 years ago and this is the first time he has missed a payment. The mortgage is now $400,000. Robert was earning about $250,000 annually. His wife earns $30,000 as a teacher. You call him 15 days after he misses the payment, optimistic that this is clearly a borrower who can get back on his feet. Unfortunately, he reports he worked for a small oil company and does not have a pension plan and has literally no savings. In addition, he has mailed 1,200 resumes attempting to find work and has not yet had one interview. A reasonable approach is to encourage him to immediately start to market his house before payments and late fees erode his interest.

The objective with the monetary defaults has not been to develop an exhaustive list of possible options. It has been to illustrate that monetary defaults vary and can be categorized. In addition to the monetary default information, all other information about the borrower, loan, collateral, metro area, payment history can be categorized. By studying and categorizing historical results considering many factors, evaluating the attempts to resolve them and the success rate of various options, you can reduce loan losses and work with borrowers more realistically. The ability to do this analysis on the fly greatly exceeds the capacity of even the brightest person.

Some of the monetary default cases will best be resolved by foreclosure. Even the permutations of handling the foreclosure can and should be studied. Some borrowers will fight you every step of the way. Some borrowers will be eager to retain their credit and be more reasonable. The borrower's history and the data you have chronicled on their monetary and non-monetary defaults will help you to understand which option makes sense.

Given the federal and state government's harsh response to foreclosing on delinquent loans, it makes sense to review options to maximize proceeds while antagonizing the borrower as little as possible. For securitized loans, there may be limits on the creativity available to quickly and cost effectively obtain possession of the collateral without motivating the borrower to trash the property.

Integrating Documents, Data, and Decision Making

Chief Data and Technology Offices are a dream hire for most companies. But compiling a big data database is only the start of solving problems. It is the development and integration of analytical and graphical tools that give direction to technicians with specialized expertise. Again, the goal is to provide distilled or filtered useful data to people making decisions. Just like a customer-service representative not having the authority to allow a short sale or restructure a loan, delivering the right information to the right people that are enabled to make the right decision is the key to growing a business. It may still require vertical business decision trees, but when all parties use and process the data effectively, better solutions are found.

Probably the most exciting aspect of big data is expediting distilled information which has been analyzed for people who can make decisions. In some cases these will be C-level executives. However, in progressive organizations, decision making will be allowed at the lowest possible level, by those who are closest to the facts and information.

Government Sponsored Entities (GSEs)

In September of 2008, the Federal Housing and Finance Agency placed Freddie Mac and Fannie Mae, two government sponsored enterprises, into conservatorship due to their poor financial status. And based on their business model they will run out of funding for operations in 2018. These two enterprises are critical to the health and financial well-being of the housing market. Do not bet against the government or Wall Street to let these two enterprises fail.

While bond investors are fighting the treasury for a portion of the cash flow from operations, the U.S. housing market needs both enterprises to help funnel the millions of new home purchases and refinances carried on every year. There are no other players in the market that can replace their financial strength.

We are Going to See a Contraction Unless Banking Regulations Change

While many of the laws enacted by the federal government after 9/11 where intended to diversify the power of big banks, those laws came with additional oversight and risk evaluation measures that smaller institutions cannot fund. The added due diligence to know your client, Patriot Act compliance, be as responsible for your vendor's actions like they are your own employees, employ internal mechanisms to keep confidential data confidential, keep misleading marketing out of the business and uphold each individual borrower as a true client relationship comes with great cost. Each and every addition caused large lenders to increase personnel to manage the actions required.

Small lenders do not have the funds necessary to hire and implement the business platforms to comply. Across the U.S., millions of borrower data is emailed, unsecure, between lender company employees, from lenders to vendors providing appraisals, survey and engineering reports and even to the borrowers themselves. And each common email carrying confidential borrower data is a violation of federal law!

The last real technology advancement in the banking world was the email system. One big bank established a protocol of encrypting emails for business, with stiff internal penalties for non-compliance. The second day after the initiative, the technology department reported 75% non-compliance and that ratio increased every day thereafter, despite threats to employees of non-compliance.

In 2014, the consumer data for 76 million of JP Morgan's clients had been found hacked. Reverberations of improper storage and lax fire walls spread across the internet, despite the company having some of the most sophisticated and advanced technology and systems in the industry. Keeping consumer data confidential is important to all businesses. Businesses are and will in increasing numbers look to enterprise storage and technology solutions, rather than customized applications that can quickly become outdated. And these enterprise applications will allow small lenders and businesses to compete with the biggest companies. However, it requires an executive management style that promotes technology. This includes e-sign, electronic documents, process-oriented applications attached to big data and the combination of young and seasoned employees working in a team approach to do their work faster and more reliably.

The property address involved in a new loan is typically entered at least 22 times throughout the lending process. A process application where the first assessment of the property search results in a property record that can then be used throughout the loan application, processing, passed on to third party vendors (appraisers, title company, environmental firms, etc.) is the key to efficiency and accuracy. This base property record is then enhanced by the borrower's contribution of corrected or missing information, pre-populates the bank-book. The application would need to auto-pull credit reports for the individual and the company, process bids and the order third party reports (appraisal, environmental, property inspection, etc.) and pre-populate closing documents in minutes, not weeks is coming soon. These efficiencies will allow mortgage bankers to process loans faster than ever before.

The Office of Comptroller of Currency (OCC) and the Federal Deposit Insurance Corporation (FDIC) expect lenders to monitor the collateral throughout the loan term. Many of those lenders have hundreds and even thousands of loans. These lenders did a whole lot of due diligence and underwriting when processing the loan, but now that it is on their books, not so much.

Loan monitoring is the next step in compliance. Assets change in value over time, as the market changes and even given varying levels of management. The level of risk / default changes over the life cycle of a loan and risk management needs to be viewed as a proactive approach.

Digital documentation and collateral underwriting of a new loan or asset will now come with periodic updates and audits that take the initial appraisal, flood status, environmental reports and property economics as autonomous reports and integrate them into a process that allows updated monitoring and risk management initiatives. Safe lending practices require continued evaluation of the asset's risk profile.

Start-Ups Focus on Special Niches

The likes of big banks and Wall Street firms have hundreds of revenue verticals (business lines collecting revenue) and generate billions of dollars in revenue. However, the thousands of start-up companies specialize in making services and technology applications better for borrowers and money exchange. Most of the successful companies will take away only a few dollars from the big boys, but the companies in aggregate will take significant revenue from individual business lines. Investment, retirement, and wealth management have historically attempted to connect investors with fund and accredited investment managers who charge periodic and buy/sell transaction fees. However, technology applications can not only speed the transaction process, but also put analytics in the hands of individuals. Sparkfund, Loannow, Wealthforge, Stockpile, and Motif Investing are but a few new entries to the market that compete with the largest financial institutions of the world for investor's dollars. The large institutions no longer compete with a regional bank expanding nationally, or an insurance company starting an investment bank; now and in the future they will have to keep up with technology changes or compete with every tech start-up that has an application to download on a smart phone and change the way investors analyze assets and make investments.

Ryan Nash and Eric Beardsley with Goldman Sachs Equity research reported that regulatory changes and new businesses with new business models are "...opening the door for an expanding class of competitors to capture profit pools long controlled by banks." Estimated at $10.9 billion, the profit pools is large and even an upstart company collecting nominal fees on transfers or processing services, if effectively scaled through mobile devices, can capture a meaningful portion of that profit pool. From 2011 to 2015, over 3,000 financial/technology start-ups and firms have raised almost $30 billion for business expansion and those firms are going after a portion of the $10.9 billion profit pool.

Organizations that play an offensive management style will do much better than those who focus on risk mitigation and defensive styles. Technology is changing so fast that focusing on calendar year budgets and planning strategies will cause firms to fall behind on the technology curve. Mergers and acquisitions between mega-conglomerates historically were considered Wall Street norms. Now, large firms need to be on the lookout for start-ups and even look to be that venture capitalist in evolving fields, like virtual reality, cognitive recognition, predictive analytics and other big data applications.

One-third of U.S. adults earn extra money through some engagement that earns them money outside of their core employment. Gallup polls reported…"87% of worldwide employees are not fully engaged at work. This is a huge loss in productivity and profits. Companies with highly engaged workforces outperform their peers by 147% in earnings per share." The prior discussion is interesting: one-third of employees are working extra jobs, but most of them are not fully engaged at work. So in order for companies to outperform their competition, their employees need to be fully engaged. And that could mean certain assignments and tasks could be delegated to part-time or seasonal employee, and even employees who work hours where they are most efficient. The hours and time standards our grandfathers worked are not the hours and time standards our younger generation are going to be bound by.

Entrepreneurs of all ages and backgrounds are building solutions to problems and making our lives more efficient. The way employees work efficiently is changing faster than any time in history. College graduates are not typically looking for 30-year careers and a pension from a single company. The idea of hierarchical management and old-school business platforms will disappear, because the younger generation does not accept the premise. They want to be engaged, excited in their work and the ability to disconnect at any time.

The elderly are participating in this entrepreneurial economy. Over 3,000,000 are self-employed. However, it requires significant knowledge to understand today's culture and implement effective business models that can scale with a growth company.

Consumer preferences are changing fast and knowing your customer is a key to success; raving fans! Digital implementation for lenders has been difficult, primarily due to the decision-makers in those companies not understanding this transformation. Decision makers need to understand that digital transformation to lead a company into the next decade first requires the knowledge of how important a digital mobile strategy is. And those applications need to be nimble, with the ability to handle changes in consumer habits. Financial technology companies are tending to focus on a singular solution, rather than a process that enhances the overall client experience. Digital banking not only needs efficiency, but also an interactive experience that invites consumers back again and again. Companies cannot underestimate that design and overall visual experience is important.

Another factor to consider is the "new currency;" bitcoin for example. The technology that monitors bitcoin transactions is Blockchain. NASDAQ is now using Ling, a Blockchain technology, to document transactions. This is a fast changing and innovative platform that will continue to undergo tremendous change. Companies wanting to grow will need to understand this environment and its applications.

Leaders in financial technology will evolve if they can:

- Provide users access to the raw data, allowing them to mine and process data as they wish,

- Lower the cost of the data with tailored subscriptions enabling users to purchase only what they need,

- Provide detailed and up-to-date contact information, and

- Provide pre-existing and customizable reports.

The commercial real estate market is estimated to total over 20 million real estate properties and the only way to lower the research and document processing cost is to "offshore" the manual portion of the processes. Quality control teams need to excel at gathering contact data, including telephone numbers, contact names, addresses, website addresses, and even the email addresses and cell phone numbers in some cases need to be verified before publishing. In addition to a highly skilled and trained research staff, there is IT infrastructure that is utilized to allocate the work-flow, track who did what research, and guide the quality control issue.

Hundreds of client and prospect meetings are needed to discuss what features, benefits and problem solving solutions are desired in business type platform, with the goal to provide not only data, but also the most efficient deliverables that real estate appraisers, brokers, lenders, investors, service providers and other professionals need in their daily work to be more efficient and make more money. For example, providing applications with data and functionality that allows appraisers to generate over half of an appraisal with auto-filled data will increase their efficiencies by over 30%.

Many company's existing infrastructure will need to be upgraded to equal or surpass the capabilities of their competitors. Many will need to be positioned for national expansion. Expect the storage needs to be at least three terabytes, but if video and photos are needed, expect at least eight terabyte storage. The established processes and procedures for researching, validating, and updating data on a continuous basis, utilizing low cost operations overseas focused on research and data verification will complete the big data process.

The Company should then position for national expansion. Senior management will need to research and develop a multi-metropolitan market business strategy for expansion. Business performance can be executed on a measured pace using existing capital or on an accelerated pace with third-party capital coupled with strategic support.

A strategic investor, with $20,000,000 of capital, can rapidly accelerate the business expansion plan. Senior management should anticipate expanding into 40 major markets within three years. Through the expansion, management should expect to find additional uses for the data as well as the need to add additional features, both of which will require minimal capital increases, but result in significant net revenue enhancements.

TREND ANALYSIS

They Are Building What? Where is the Money Coming From?

"If you can't make it here, you can't make it anywhere"

- Ed Wulfe, Chairman & CEO of Wulfe & Company

In 2014, Texas' major markets were expanding at levels unseen anywhere else in the U.S. and, this time, it was not a speculative-driven market. The negative economic forces hindering recovery in the rest of the country were absent in Texas, resulting in a building boom locally. Because there were hundreds of new projects springing up across the state, we want to just showcase an overall summary of the magnitude of the development schedules.

UNDER CONSTRUCTION								
	Apartments		Industrial		Office		Retail	
	Projects	Units	Projects	Sq Ft	Projects	Sq Ft	Projects	Sq Ft
Austin	44	11,966	10	1,546,427	8	604,005	12	2,245,903
Dallas	57	15,107	13	5,240,826	36	5,925,711	40	6,502,813
Houston	47	12,701	24	2,464,634	25	3,499,081	34	4,210,032
San Antonio	12	2,844	11	2,585,743	11	908,527	12	1,686,027
Total	**160**	**42,618**	**58**	**11,837,630**	**80**	**10,937,324**	**98**	**14,644,775**

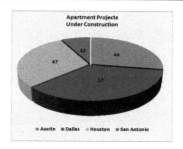

Source: www.enricheddata.com

It is obvious that at this time in the market all segments of the commercial real estate market in the Texas major metro areas are experiencing substantial expansion. Some examples of the new development are:

Houston

In 2013 expect:

- Two new Kroger's and an expansion of existing store

- One new Whole Foods Market

- One new HEB supermarket

- One Trader Joe's

- Newcomers Sprouts and Fresh Market, four each
- ALDI with fifteen new stores
- Two new Walmart Super Centers
- Two Sam's Clubs
- Ross three new stores
- Marshall's, Steinmart, one each
- Three new theaters
- 22-screen Santikos Paladium theater
- Bellfort, a 12-screen Cinemark
- Studio Movie Grill in League City
- Two new Costco stores
- DD's Discount

Let us talk CBD; after 5 million square feet of leasing in 2012 and one of the highest square foot office prices ever paid for an office building in the state, big projects are underway.

- Capitol Tower
- 397-unit, 7-story apartment property
- SkyHouse Houston, a $60+ million, 24-floor, 336-unit residential tower
- 1,000-room Marriott Marquis.

With a great recent history of increased rents, pricing and occupancy, what in the world could go wrong? How about $40 per barrel oil? Who would have ever predicted the world's oil supply would move to an over-supply position and cause prices to drop from over $100 per barrel, to around $40 in a matter of a few short months? Where oil-related jobs are a significant segment of the economy, layoffs of $300,000+ salaried employees became an everyday occurrence. New buildings stood empty and employment growth dropped to less than 20% of previous years. Upscale restaurant attendance dropped significantly.

Could big data predictive analytics have predicted that this could happen? It is a great question. No local, regional or national economist could have predicted this, because they did not have access to the big data necessary to run the decision trees that would filter the necessary answers. With hundreds of millions of dollars in overbuilt inventory, Wall Street and big banks certainly should have data and tools required to properly evaluate real estate markets and predictive analytics to help foresee market occurrences.

Big Data Analytics

While new technology devices drive increases in data creation, the data needs to be standardized and filtered before it can be meaningful. Unfortunately, most of this data is being neglected. Large data sets that cannot be processed into meaningful trends, or that cannot help answer fundamental questions, or help businesses achieve newfound successes, are useless. Big data related to the real estate industry comes from:

- County Tax Rolls
- Deeds of Trust (recording of a lien / mortgage)
- Deeds (recording of a sale)
- Business Filings (Comptroller of Currency)
- Title Companies (refinancing / sales)
- Q10 Filings from Public Companies
- Real Estate Investment Trust (REIT) Reporting

Interviews and surveys with:
- Owners
- Sellers
- Appraisers
- Property Managers
- Property Inspectors
- Leasing Agents
- Real Estate Brokers

So how can a simple Case Shiller Index, a 20-city composite of home prices, be used to measure the health of the housing market? According to the February 2015 Case Shiller report:

> "The S&P/Case-Shiller Home Price Indices are designed to be a reliable and consistent benchmark of housing prices in the United States. Their purpose is to measure the average change in home prices in a particular geographic market. They are calculated monthly and cover 20 major metropolitan areas (Metropolitan Statistical Areas or MSAs), which are also aggregated to form two composites – one comprising 10 of the metro areas, the other comprising all 20.
>
> The indices measure changes in housing market prices given a constant level of quality. Changes in the types

and sizes of houses or changes in the physical characteristics of houses are specifically excluded from the calculations to avoid incorrectly affecting the index value."

"This methodology was created by S&P Dow Jones Indices to achieve the aforementioned objective of measuring the underlying interest of each index governed by this methodology document. Any changes to or deviations from this methodology are made in the sole judgment and discretion of S&P Dow Jones Indices so that the index continues to achieve its objective."

Appraisers sometimes use matched-pairs analysis to support the "value" of a component in a house, like a pool. Two identical homes that sell at similar times, but one with a pool and another without, are compared to each other and the variance in pricing is assumed to be the "value" of the pool; Although, value is not price! And value is not cost! While that pool may cost $26,000 to install, the "value" of the pool when sold with the house, is typically less than $26,000; sometimes even $10,000 to $15,000 less. This matched-pairs analysis can be used to measure a number of house components:

- Homes with a new roof versus those with a 20-year old roof;

- Homes with upgraded bathrooms;

- Homes the sale size, but one has three-bedrooms and the other has four;

- Homes with two car detached garages versus those with a carport.

While larger sampling sets provide increased reliability, the Case Shiller index attempts to match pairs of pre-existing homes (no new homes are included) to arrive at a consistent way to measure index value.

	EffectiveDate	Index Level	1 MTH	3 MTH	12 MTH
INDEX LEVELS					
S&P/Case-Shiller 20-City Composite Home Price Index	Mar-2016	184.50	0.90 %	1.10 %	5.43 %

AS OF MAR 2016

The Index is reported to be the most accurate way to look at home price appreciation in a city; between cities and in markets they cover.

Unique Internal and External Influences

Let's look at the San Francisco Bay and Silicon Valley housing market.

The Bay Area's tech driving market is leading to a rebounding economy. Based on what we knew in the first half of 2014, year-end 2014 employment growth is expected to exceed the 2013 total. In fact, during the entire period for which county level employment data was available at that time, dating back to 1970, the city has never seen a more rapid three-year period of expansion in jobs than the period between 2010 and 2013.

The region's growth is led by tech industry expansion, fueled by new initial public offerings (IPO), the first sale of stock by a private company to the public, and venture capital investments. IPOs are often issued by smaller, younger companies seeking the capital to expand, but can also be done by large privately owned companies looking to become publicly traded. Wealthy investors or crowd funding from qualified investors (singles with incomes over $250,000, married with incomes over $350,000, or $1,000,000 net worth, excluding your home) provide money called Venture Capital to startup firms and small businesses, most who are targeting significantly high growth potential. Both IPO's and Venture Capitalists are important funding sources for many technology based companies.

Venture capital investment totaled around $28 billion in 2013 across the U.S. and the Bay Area captured around 46% of the investment. Mergers and acquisitions has also surged, with some very impressive valuations in the tech sector, such as Facebook's $19 billion purchase of 50-person What's App.

In 2013, 220 IPO deals included the $2.3 billion Twitter deal, which created 1,600 millionaires in the San Francisco Bay area alone. The Bay Area has exceeded all other areas of the country in attracting IPO capital, with 13% (26% for all of California) of the investments coming to the region.

For the months following the Twitter IPO funding, upper end house prices jumped as much as 35%! That is what new wealth families tend to do, spend money on luxury items that they could never afford before. That 30-year old techie who purchased that $4,000,000 2,400 square foot condominium does not really care about the above market price, it is about the lifestyle.

Research Division of the National Association of REALTORS®, in cooperation with the Florida REALTORS®, conducted an annual survey of purchases of existing homes by international clients since 2005 and found:

> Florida is one of the major U.S. destinations of international residential real estate buyers. Approximately 25 percent of foreign home buyers purchasing U.S. property buy Florida properties.

Interesting findings in the report show how important international buyers are to the community:

- International unit sales totaled 44,000 properties, 12 percent of Florida's residential market (15 percent a year prior), compared to four percent nationally.

- The dollar volume of international sales totaled $23.7 billion, 24 percent of Florida's residential dollar volume of sales (19 percent a year ago), compared to eight percent nationally.

- Respondents reported a significant increase in the share of buyers from Latin America to 56 percent (23 percent a year ago).

- Foreigners purchased property at the average price of $538,600 ($300,600 in 2014), compared to the median price of Florida's residential sales of $258,200. The substantial change in average price appears to be due to market mix.

Let's examine the last two findings.

Buyers from Latin America increased their share from 23 percent to 56 percent in one year and a good percentage of those are wealthy business people wishing to relocate as a result of security and financial concerns in their country of origin. And based on international buyers purchasing homes twice as high as the median price for the state, these buyers are pushing upper end pricing.

Since foreign buyers are so prevalent in the market, do the lenders and appraisers have a big data tool that helps them measure the economics of not only the South Florida market, but also the countries from where most of these buyers are coming from? Could buyers being purchasing in Florida because their home country has political or economic turbulence? Do international buyers have a potentially higher foreclosure rate than U.S. nationals? These are all great questions that need to be answered before millions of lending dollars are concentrated in this market.

For a decade prior to 2016, wealthy Texans were purchasing some of the most exclusive and expensive homes in the Rocky Mountains. Prices in Aspen and Vale continued to climb as Texas attorneys, oil barons, and business executives bought log cabin mansions, pushing prices upward and the locals to lower-priced, smaller homes. The marginal pay at local jobs caused locals to speak unkindly to and about their cowboy boot-wearing visitors.

Even in 2015, when oil prices declined, 22 of the 48 home purchases above $500,000 in Pagosa Springs area of Southwest Colorado came from Texans. And those homes sold at slightly less than $1 million each. There are few jobs in Pagosa Springs that allow a local to purchase these homes.

So whether internal community influences like IPOs and venture capitalists, or external influences like wealthy international buyers and Texans, simple house pricing indexes do not tell real estate investors and homeowners sufficient information to strategically evaluate buy and sell decisions. There is no doubt that a decline in these internal and external influences will depress pricing in those markets. And when that occurs, the contrarian investor should look hard at the depressed pricing opportunities.

Similar to the struggle individual investors in the stock market have deciding to buy or sell when the market is going up or down; -look to buy in a stock market going up and sell in a market going down, they do not have the institutional tools or the speed of execution to compete with institutional Wall Street firms.

But in the real estate world, the clarity needed to evaluate market trends and act on those trends is more of a level playing field for the individual and the larger institutional level; at least in the lower end pricing real estate market. Bidding at auctions or making offers on listings that just went on the market that are available to anyone with the fortitude to understand their market better than anyone else is a key to success.

Predictive analytics is just an idea in most organizations. Advanced forms of predictive analytics allow companies to foresee changes coming to their industry. And no industry needs it more than the financial market, particularly in lending. While the number of (25,000+) Class A apartment units built and under construction in Houston may not have been the sole factor in over-building, the decline of oil prices to under $50 certainly fueled the fire. Six months free rent, rental rates per square foot at 60% of projections, and oil company layoffs contribute to the anticipated foreclosures in the Houston apartment market in latter 2016 and into 2017. With so many smart people in the real estate and financial markets, how could this happen?

Knowing the social habits of those residents occupying new apartments is very important to making predictive analytics. The percentage of renters using the workout room and pool, whether they refer their friends as new residents, if they need two parking spaces rather than one, if they bike, and if they work at home or commute are all data points to be collected. There is a need to know which new apartments are faring the best in tough times; those in urban versus suburban locations, apartments next to a park, and those adjacent to public transportation versus those requiring car travel to work are all important factors. It becomes a more controlled environment when considering mixed use developments encompassing retail and office space where granular data points are processed throughout the project. Detailed data points allow big data to provide predictive analytical conclusions.

Combining public and private data needs to have that socio-economic input to allow predictive analytics to be processed. The data inputs need to consider at least 10-years of history and the longer the better. Predictive analytics also needs to incorporate machine learning and artificial intelligence. The data can then be processed to not only provide a clear picture of the asset and the investment (credit and trend risk, historical capital improvements, environmental issues, tenant's ability to pay and budget / cash flow projections), but also external influences like interest rates, employment and population for the community, income levels, construction prices, under and proposed construction trends and projections. Predictive analytics allows a clearer picture of the future of real estate, finance and investment. Investors need these tools to be at the forefront of making prudent investment decisions. And those analytics will open up new business opportunities.

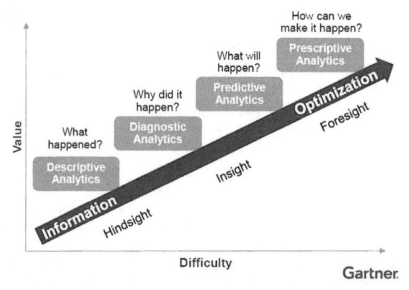

However, most companies fall into data overload and inability to effectively process this data. Business and financial leaders tend to rely on their work history and less on technology applications in making the business decisions for their company. But there is no better time to bring those young professionals into decision making positions and help companies redirect their decisions in order to grow in the upcoming decades. One of the first business decisions is to hire the right people that could have a substantially different background than the professionals currently in the organization.

A mortgage brokerage firm with six seasoned mortgage bankers can be hugely complemented by bringing in an associated arts graduate with analytical and social media skills. The newbie can process data and trends to provide insight into borrower's actions, concerns and motivations. Interpreting social media trends is a lot easier and insightful when analyzed by a professional who is actively using the technology.

The ability to contract technology experts is easier than ever. Whether building customized websites or code programming to develop new products and applications, the web provides numerous outlets for hire. A search for "Hire Tech Talent" in Google returns 3.9 million results.

An organizational change also needs to be incorporated into a business platform to effectively employ predictive analytics. Client management systems allow management to evaluate how effective the business tools and producers are. Providing business opportunities to those individuals who are better at engaging in phone conversations, versus those individuals active in social media platforms is a management decision one uses to be most effective. And gaining new business today requires multiple touch points; mass marketing, target marketing, social media connections, attending seminars and conventions complement the history of lunch meetings and golf outings with clients.

New, low cost, servers or cloud applications storing historical enriched data by a company is an asset that can be valued and monetized. However, once it is downloaded onto a professional's private computer (PC), enhancements and the ability to analyze and use that data for the overall good of the company is lost. That is why cloud and enterprise applications are being used by growing companies. Meshing multiple data points into records where specific data important to a business's success can then be extracted and fed to those professionals in the driver's seat and makes them more money.

With the right talent, an organization willing to embrace technology applications and predictive analytics allows companies to focus on the data points that are most important to sustaining and growing their business. A home-builder focusing on a single market is going to need a part-time job or be willing to relocate when cyclical real estate downturns occur. Real estate investors will have limited opportunities to purchase properties at a discount when the pricing cycle is peaking. The ability to focus on construction, price, foreclosure, interest and rental rate trends in multiple markets provides a dashboard that is important to real estate investors.

Like no time in the past, retailers with physical store operations are competing with on-line purchasing. Those retailers need to retool and focus their marketing and physical presence to attract consumers who want to comingle in areas outside their home. While retailers tend to mass-market sales on holiday weekends, weather can have a measurable effect on retail sales. Retailers who evaluate weather patterns can focus sales on days when their consumers favor store visits.

Even in the real estate business, the data on consumer behavior is more important than that of the base real estate data. Property details have historically been the focus of big data in real estate, but data that can be used for predictive analytics allows companies to be out in front of new trends.

Predictive analytics can then feed prescriptive analytics, how companies can influence current and prospective clients to interact with products and services. Predicting who and why people open a certain email, click on a link, buy a product and go to a retailer's store, overlaid with local economic factors and even weather patterns and trends allows retailers to influence consumers to buy. The idea of a college student ordering fast food through a food delivery service would have never been given a thought 10 years ago. Why someone would not want to get up and go through a drive-thru is something most of us would never build a business around. But that new business line, even for a $5 happy meal, can entice thousands of other college students to make the delivery for $3 to the college client who is willing to pay $8 to have a happier meal!

The real estate agent and brokerage community has historically been the focus of big data aggregation in real estate. With big data, agents and brokers only need a "slice" of the data and need that data delivered in a manner that makes them more productive. While many internet deliverables provide free access, those websites are collecting information on a consumer's profile. Strategically focusing the data in a deliverable to professionals in action (those that will actually do something with the data) is the key to increasing income. And strategic marketing is required to attract those "action" users to the platform. When effective data and analytics is delivered to action users, both the number of deals and the profitability per deal is increased.

Built-Out Community

A built-out community is a place where there is no more land for expansion. On Jan. 16, 2005, Peter Corbett of The Arizona Republic wrote an article:

"Out of Land And Water, Scottsdale Is Built Out"

A golfing mecca for the rich, Scottsdale went on a building boom. The first subdivision in the Southwest U.S., Desert Mountain commanded $1,000,000 lot prices and golf courses using 1 million gallons of water per day. However, a national forest on its northern boundary, City of Tempe to the south, City of Phoenix to the west and the Pima Indian Reservation to the east, the city ran out of land to annex. And then developers ran out of land to build on.

Scottsdale, AZ

Acres of Buildable Developed

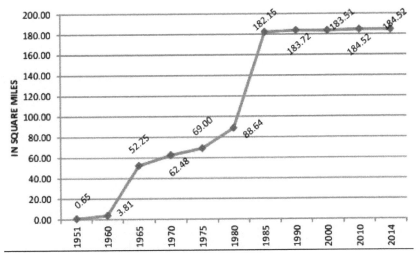

Source: City of Scottsdale

Hundreds and even thousands of desert acres covered with cactus and desert flowers were being put into real estate development production each year. From about 1998 to 2000, the built out acreage plus the amount of acreage being built on each year could be calculated and a projection of community built-out from 2005 to 2007 could easily be determined.

And let's go back and look at San Francisco, which has been built-out for decades. Aspen and Vail have had similar lack of land. In the last decade, Salt Lake City also essentially reached build-out and those subdivisions near Deer Valley and Park City ski areas started selling for over $1,000,000. When communities reach build-out, increased appreciation occurs. And that bodes well for investors!

Once Scottsdale achieved build-out, homeowners experienced some of the highest home price appreciation every recorded. Home values doubled in less than 10 years. Homeowners where getting home equity loans to buy beachfront property in San Diego and bungalows in sleepy Mexico fishing villages like Puerto Penasco (Rocky Point).

Find a community that is nearing build-out and you should see a near term "pop" in appreciation once it occurs!

WHAT THE FUTURE HOLDS

In the 2016 presidential election, we all saw how media hype can tend to exaggerate the gravity of the situation. So how do we extract data that is relevant and meaningful? Let us look at some examples of trends that will help mold the future.

Information has been called the next great natural resource. Today's emergence of big data fuels the base of significant opportunity to support smarter management of facilities; everything from office buildings to retail stores, hospitals and schools. The ability to effectively channel and analyze the massive amounts of data generated from facilities can help increase revenue, power operational efficiency, ensure service availability and mitigate risk.

There is nothing wrong with relying on third-party vendors as the basis for your data. But know what you are getting:

- Has there been any third-party verification of the public data?

- Are the phone numbers purchased from a massive data warehouse (like White Pages) or are they independently verified as accurate?

- Do you have email addresses? Did anyone check to see if they are accurate and up to date?

- Have you connected the person to their LinkedIn or Facebook account?

- How often is the data updated?

An important feature of data collection and updating is the enhancement of information by an internal network of employees, venders and other third-party data collectors. A national network of data collectors can provide field confirmations, enhancing the data so it provides the most thorough and accurate information.

Using unique database abilities with the objective being to isolate judgments that a party had made in the past can then be used to help isolate predictive factors. Let us examine real estate auction sales. One would think that this is a great place to buy underpriced real estate assets. However, the possibility that the seller may provide a clouded title or secondary liens not related to the foreclosure adds certain risk. Knowing how often the seller sells at an auction and the historical pricing to market value, gives you the ability to quickly and efficiently evaluate liens and clouds on titles. One of the largest secondary lien researchers in the U.S. evaluated over 24,000 non-exempt (non-homestead) liens in order to make offers on 520 properties and successfully purchase 419 of them, which allowed the researcher a cost basis at a fraction of the market value. With annual yields of 15% to 35%, this division has tremendous growth potential and is one of the only companies in the U.S. with the ability to effectively and efficiently research judgments, acquires them and converts the judgment to a real estate lien for faster-leveraged collections.

Another factor is the extensive contact information published for the buyer, seller, lender, broker representative, property manager or property contact (address, phone and in most cases, email address). This essentially creates a "LinkedIn" of real estate investors and contacts active in the commercial real estate world. Also, knowledge of how many people are in any retail store or office building at any one time is now available, and the app tracks cell phone locations! This creates a "live" database that literally changes every second.

Competitive Environment for Market Research Data

Numerous vendors provide market research and others provide applications that use and process data. However, applications attached to big data databases are keys to providing fast, accurate and efficient solutions to problems. Firms that provide statistics, data or even transactional information require their clients to download the data and process the information that they need. The market is moving to national real estate and people databases connected to thousands of applications. Users enhance the data both while they use the data and in their everyday work and social activities. Nothing can replace enriched data that has reliable information.

"Intellectual property has the shelf life of a banana."

- Bill Gates

Land can be transformed from native pastures to cities of skyscrapers and even epic buildings have "shelf lives" that require renovation or even demolition. The core asset, land or buildings to be razed, will be the next acquisition target in growth markets. Employment, population and housing growth are drivers of urban sprawl and revitalization of urban cores, pushing the land development "button," But as every real estate professional has been told, "The three most important factors in buying are: location, location, and location."

Employment growth will spur additional home demand and that will spur new construction. As it takes about one to two years to buy a piece of land, get it entitled, establish utility districts and start construction of homes or mixed use development; a shortage of home inventory in Austin and Houston, and possibly Dallas, will be very evident as we go through the coming years. This will spur demand for land, both developable and pre-developable.

Funding for land development will be strictly limited to well-capitalized developers, particularly those with significant equity. Highway expansions will pave the way for new submarket locations and retail development will follow new rooftops. Existing planned unit developments touted as live/work/play environments will see above-average residential, commercial and business park demand, if in down markets.

And the success of new projects will be driven by, what else, location!

"I don't measure a man's success by how high he climbs, but how high he bounces when he hits bottom."

- General George S. Patton

Real estate markets throughout the U.S. have cyclical trends that have highs and lows. In declining markets, regional markets tend to bounce back differently. Those that had the highest appreciation bounce the most – California, South Florida, Las Vegas, and Arizona. Those that have moderate appreciation prior to a downturn bounce the least – Texas, Mid-West, third and secondary cities. But even the most expensive U.S. cities have a long way to go to make the World's Most Expensive markets!

Top Ten - Most Expensive Office Markets		
Rank	Location	Cost/SF
1	Hong Kong (Central), Hong Kong	$235.23
2	London - Central (West End), United Kingdom	$222.58
3	Beijing (Finance Street), China	$195.07
4	Beijing (CBD), China	$187.06
5	New Delhi (Connaught Place - CBD), India	$178.96
6	Hong Kong (West Kowloon), Hong Kong	$173.90
7	Moscow, Russian Federation	$165.05
8	Tokyo (Marunouchi/Otemachi), Japan	$161.16
9	London - Central (City), United Kingdom	$132.94
10	New York (Midtown Manhattan),U.S.	$120.65

From some strange reason, bragging about a mortgage rate takes on such status as how far one can hit a baseball or how big the fish was"

- David Reed, CD Reed

Too Much of a Good Thing May Be a Bad Thing

When taking a drink of water, lighting a match, or flying a kite, most people do not stop and think about how a substance or action that can be very beneficial to an individual or society can also cause significant destruction. While water is the staff of life, it also causes billions of dollars in flooding and other drainage disasters on a yearly basis. Fire is a major force when controlled, but also causes incredible disasters. One can conclude that the overabundance or improper usage of a good thing can clearly present negative forces if improperly applied or applied in an excessive amount.

While interest rate levels are clearly a man-made phenomenon and not subject to nature, they are affected by the concepts of overabundance and distortion. Low interest rates have become a part of our economy; however, this artificially low term structure has afforded many households the ability to purchase or refinance a home on beneficial terms. In effect, like a hurricane promotes its own weather system, a sustained lower term structure of interest rates has promoted its own economic system. But this economic environment, in addition to fostering additional growth, enjoyment, consumption and investment, has created its own system, and lacks policies with a safety net. Parties involved in the capital markets are not prepared for a shift (increase) in rates.

Too often, like the calm before the storm, individuals or corporations become comfortable with an economic scenario that is known to be unsustainable over the medium or longer terms. Presently, corporations have utilize low interest rates to incur substantial debt, allowing stock buybacks, and many households have followed a similar pattern with their real estate home equity loans and increases in credit card debt. While this might be good for individual corporations or households, it is probably not beneficial for the overall fiber of our society; namely, the fallacy of composition - the false assumption that what is true for a part will also be true for the whole.

As interest rates have maintained their historically low levels, of course created by artificial means, few people are prepared for the storm after the calm. Many are projecting that the storm will either never come or come at such a reduced level it is not worth undertaking programs to soften the blow. The multiplier effect of the storm, namely the consequential effects, have not been fully explored or stated in our national economic press. True, a future storm could be considered a weak one if it only affected a small part or segment of our economic system. However, rising rates will not occur in a vacuum. Rising rates in one sector will clearly have a pronounced effect on other sectors, with all coming together at roughly the same time.

Rising rates might have an initial effect upon reducing home sales, corporate capital investments and refinancing of capital assets. These actions, when accompanied by sustained cuts in all levels of government spending and potentially increased operational fees (or taxes), will only serve to make adverse effects more concentrated, focused and intense. Increasing interest rates usually leads to acquisition cutbacks that often promote increased "blue collar" unemployment and decreased consumer consumption, which can further decrease employment levels and subsequently lower consumption. While this cycle in prior times has been broken by lowering interest rates and/or increased government expenditures, these two options would not be available in a near term cycle.

So what should we do when taxing agencies go overboard? Let's consider Philadelphia, where the Actual Value Initiative ("AVI") started in 2010 resulted in the first major real estate property reassessment in several decades of all 579,000 parcels in the City of Philadelphia. Not only has the city lost millions from its lack of annual reassessment in an appreciating market, but homeowners, building owners and tenants are going to be hit with significant expense increases.

The data collected by assessors throughout the U.S. is not necessarily the best data to use for predictive analytics. The data tends to be static, does not have a sufficient number of data fields and tends to have inaccuracies. Data results that tell a story and provide real-time accuracy are of the most value to a company and its professionals.

While increased rates will afford debt instrument holders increased rates of return, holding those instruments in an environment of a rising interest rates could result in capital loss, in addition to lost opportunity costs. Since the day of increasing interest rates is only a matter of weeks or months (not years or decades) ahead, a productive investor needs to remain flexible, liquid and creative in order to capitalize on future investment opportunities. The inability to restructure corporate debt or an investment portfolio of stocks, bonds, real estate and even commodities could become not only a mistake, but also an error that affects rate of return beyond the next economic cycle.

The next economic cycle will surely be different than most, if not all, cycles from times past. A changing interest rate environment will require those investing in the next economic cycle to not only think "outside of the box" but also to create new boxes to maintain healthy returns. Investors will be encouraged to take risk and reward by seeking investments that will further reinforce a more solid structure of interest rates which would also allow for and foster long-term growth. Such might be the answer for investment into different levels of efficiency that could allow our nation to once again become self-sustaining – as opposed to having a somewhat flat level of interest rate rewards and a rather flat economy.

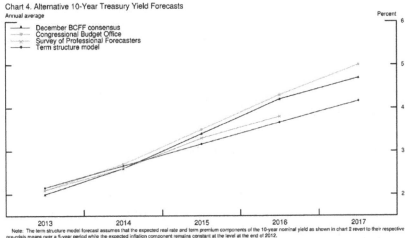

Chart 4. Alternative 10-Year Treasury Yield Forecasts
Annual average

Percent

- December BCFF consensus
- Congressional Budget Office
- Survey of Professional Forecasters
- Term structure model

Note: The term structure model forecast assumes that the expected real rate and term premium components of the 10-year nominal yield as shown in chart 2 revert to their respective pre-crisis means over a 5-year period while the expected inflation component remains constant at the level at the end of 2012.
Source: For December BCFF consensus, Blue Chip Financial Forecasts (BCFF) survey, December 2012; for Congressional Budget Office, Congressional Budget Office (2013), *The Budget and Economic Outlook: Fiscal Years 2013 to 2023* (Washington: CBO), February 5; for Survey of Professional Forecasters, Survey of Professional Forecasters for 2013:Q1.

Bond rates and pricing are as important to real estate economics as interest rates are to loans. Municipalities and governments sell bonds to fund all types of real estate projects and other endeavors, such as hospitals, low income housing, water districts (clean drinking water is a key to a community's prosperity), and roads. Bond traders look for opportunities where a low bond price today could have sufficient upside to make the investment. Many times, municipal bonds use taxes to pay back those bond issuances.

Let us assume a new master-planned community is being built. The developer will get approval and issue a municipal utility district bond (MUD) specifically to develop clean water and a process plant to re-circulate water and sewer runoff. Projections are made as to the growth in the assessed values (tax base) and how the resulting taxes will pay off those bonds over time. Say $8,000,000 worth of water and sewer district improvements are needed; the bonds would be sold and as new homes connect to the water and sewer plants, a 'tap-in' fee typically would be charged to cover a portion of the capital infrastructure. An additional tax rate (say MUD #33 District Rate) would be assessed to those new homes in the area. The tax payments would be used to pay off those bonds over, say the next 20 years. Whether building real estate with government-backed bonds, or water/sewer district improvements, the process is fundamentally the same.

The investors in those bonds over the next 20 years may change. Some may hold the entire term, but many of the initial investors will sell the bonds before the maturity date. Those bonds then get re-priced based on a number of factors, how much demand there is for bonds at that time, any external influences affecting pricing; and other factors. Bond traders put a weighted-average risk profile together for each bond; sometimes at a discount (more risky), sometimes at par (same price as issuance) and sometimes at a premium (less risk). Bonds are typically priced to the event which is nearest to payoff; a five year call.

The health of the real estate-backed bonds in your local market is an important consideration when evaluating commercial real estate. Look at Puerto Rico's recent non-payment of their bond obligations. The affects are widespread and trickle down to each resident, taxpayer, real estate owner and investor. That single event can have adverse effects on investment real estate demand and pricing. Investors needed to not only look at Puerto Rico's ability to pay its bonds, but should have also evaluated the Teachers Retirement System (TRS), public-employee pensions and the Employees Retirement System (ERS) obligations. With over 300,000 employees and retirees in the system, there is only $1.8 billion in funds to pay for over $43 billion in liabilities.

As economies deteriorate due to the heavy burden of debt and unfunded obligations, the weight falls on the community's residents. And they will not take it lightly. There is nothing more energizing to policemen, schoolteachers, and fire fighters than spending a 30-year career expecting a pension and ending up penniless. They will, no doubt, go to the streets, the voting booths, and the media to let government officials, who may be blameless at that time, know they are considered to be at fault.

What about when a large corporation with 10-year tax breaks decides after three years that they want to relocate and vacate that new $500,000,000 plant. Not only is there three years of lost taxes, regional relocations that previously occurred to satisfy job demand and likely increased government spending on other areas of the community (schools, social benefits), there is the drag on the economy that can bankrupt a community, again affecting each resident, taxpayer, real estate owner and investor in that community.

Promises made by municipalities trying to woo Corporate America can backfire and bring on an evolution which could result in worse economic conditions than before. The idea of incentives is only good if both parties carry through, and Corporate America, for some reason or another, may not be able to carry through on its end of the agreement. Promises of tax abatements or even forgiveness can accelerate employment growth, which may not be sustainable.

But politicians want to get elected and businesses want to make money. Transparency in government and real estate financial stability or instability needs to go hand-in-hand. The level of municipal bonds, taxation on real estate, and other factors need to be transparent to investors who purchase those bonds, but also to the community at large.

Want to Manage Big Data

The U.S. Bureau of Labor Statistics in 2016 reported that network systems and data communications analyst will be the fastest-growing career with a 53.4% increase in employment and an average salary of $67,460. The analyst position typically requires a bachelor's degree. And relevant work experience is a key to moving up the ladder. Businesses are continuing to purchase and implement new technology and network systems.

Companies that want to manage big data will not only require new talent and the infrastructure needed to manage and process structured and unstructured data, but will need to conduct this analysis with high security features. There are substantial threats throughout the world that want your big data and do not want to put in the time and effort big data companies have done to get it legally.

Servers in your office (although some people keep them in their bathroom or basement) may be a thing of the past, as cloud computing is making way for massive cloud storage. This is allowing for not only upgrade efficiencies, but also lower costs of operations and faster results. Once the challenge of data storage and processing is achieved, firms will need to continue the evolution of capturing the data which is important to them and their business.

Real-Time Analysis

Data can pile up quicker than wine bottles at a Napa Valley convention. As data comes in, sophisticated algorithms and programs are used to process that data quicker than ever. Distributed systems, rather than rigid data tables or other architecture structures, provides for easier real time analysis. Warehousing data will soon be a thing of the past. Analyzing data at the point of sale is a key to working with current trends and gives firms the ability to project future trends.

Big data, processed in simple deliverables to experienced professionals in the field, allows them to interact with customers and prospects to deliver best-in-class experience. Coupled with the age old adage, "people do business with people they like," the ability for even small entrepreneurs to conduct business with high dollar customers changes the global business environment.

The days of a middle merchant traveling to Spain to meet with a 10th generation wine maker to market that product to sophisticated sommeliers is in the past. Organic farmers from around the world can reach out to the HEBs involved in massive grocery markets and sell direct. Point of sale contact (e-check, PayPal, Authorize.net, etc.) make every product originator a mass marketer, if they use the right tools.

In a digital economy, there is no state, national, cultural or ethnic boundaries. Interactions occur in real-time. Mastery of scale is based on individual and company drive; no longer will firewalls restrict access. Global data is assembled at a prodigious rate and every person and company can access data equally, if they have the technology proficiencies. Big data, simplified!

Six-month-old data will no longer be valid, but point of contact data showing why yesterday an international homebuyer paid $380,000 for a home in an off-market transaction while a local Floridian offering $330,000 for the same house on the same street, will be important. The future will view real time analytics and sophisticated analysis to interpret that data and deliver simple solutions to the producers in the field. Firms would have never thought of the capabilities just a few years ago.

A new homebuilder could evaluate not only the buying trends of existing homeowners at the local home improvement stores, but also track what colors of paint they buy, whether hardwood or tile is preferred and the styles of ceiling fans, appliances and furniture replacements. Empirical models that measure the cost-benefit analysis for home upgrades (typically carpet, bedroom and baths) above 'standard' finishes is also important to let selling brokers know which upgrades to push the hardest.

Real estate brokers would very much appreciate the opportunity to know when homeowners in their community become empty-nesters. Finding clients who are downsizing from those large suburban homes is a huge win for brokers, as they can initiate both the sell and buy side for the empty-nesters. Tying college freshman coming in from out of town to their parent's home address is a straightforward process.

With smart phones now being the common denominator for almost everyone in America, there is a strong likelihood that our phone number will carry though our entire lifetime. That 8-year old who just received their first phone for their birthday will most likely have that cell number for the next 90 years!

Don't like to cold call? Embrace emails and social media. Connect to your targeted prospects via LinkedIn, Facebook, Twitter, etc. If you like to call, then you are ahead of the game. While cold calling may be the most grim act most people can think of doing, connecting with a prospect to build a long term relationship is the key to a successful business. Even if that prospect will never buy your product, a sphere of like-kind networks builds brand awareness and may lead to other opportunities. Having a prospect introduce you to another prospect allows you an easier introduction and continues to build your brand. Brand awareness is as important as an effective sales team.

Retailers who can reach out to those people who are a hot lead will change the way retailers interact with potential clients. Imagine a couple who saved for a year for their dream island vacation, but the cost of massages is a little outside of their budget. To increase business the island spa during low periods of use could ping the cell phones of the couples that walk by that store for the next hour with the message "massages are half price for the next 30 minutes." The retailer would change the way they historically interact with potential clients and maximize revenue by instigating interaction with prospects they know are in the area. Everyone now has a cell phone and they know where you are!

Investors looking for triple net NNN purchases have minimal data requirements in order to determine buy decisions. Conversely, purchasing a 500-unit apartment complex or 100-tenant retail / office development requires much more sophisticated underwriting. If investors could purchase investment real estate that has minimal management requirements for the same capitalization rate as complex multi-tenant assets, why would they not purchase the triple net NNN asset? Well, the downside of a tenant vacating a triple net NNN asset is a lot higher than even a few tenants vacating a 500-unit apartment complex.

But if every triple net, NNN asset in the U.S. could be ranked, sorted and given a weighting scale by: traffic counts, sales per square foot, year built, remaining lease term, ratio of price to building cost plus land value, and credit strength of the tenant; an investor would make a better-informed decision. Excluding the credit strength of the tenant, the other factors would equalize the comparison and a push towards the highest capitalization rates would prevail. Even if vacancy occurs, locations with high traffic counts and sales per square foot, plus newer-year built assets, are likely to be released quickly.

Investors should gravitate to Tier 2 and even Tier 3 cities to obtain the highest yields, as many times there is a 50 to 150 basis point increase in the capitalization rate versus the same type of building in a Tier 1 city. There is much more competition in Tier 1 cities for real estate investment, tending to push down yields.

Systems

With millions growing to billions of machines being connected to the internet, the physical and digital world will converge in databases and sophisticated computer programs allowing almost anyone anywhere in the world access to real-time results. Those programs will think faster than humans on how to improve the search results. Users will be able to focus on data analysis. Flexible data processing will be needed to properly filter those few data points important to the real estate professional, investor or lender. Programmers and developers directed by high-level chief information officers looking for business solutions to direct business expansion will be at the forefront of these useful technologies.

Enterprise systems using data will rely on larger big data providers. Architecture surrounding these systems will continue to evolve and new hardware servers will quickly be outdated, many in just a couple of years. The cost of cloud computing and data storage and processing will decrease while the speed of delivery will increase.

While large corporations build proprietary systems to enable their businesses to run faster and to reach more customers, there will be few mass-marketed products that will allow for customization catering to the specific needs of the small business and individual consumer. Those businesses and consumers will need to modify their business platforms in order to achieve growth opportunities.

The days of the "click fee" and monthly reoccurring charges are here to stay. Big data providers want and need sustainable revenue streams, with new applications offered with add-on fees and enterprise solutions requiring gold and platinum subscription rates. Marketing through these technology applications will drive to a point of sale process, reaching prospective clients when they are in the area of a retailer or service provider or reach out to individuals that are conducting internet searches. Those searches trigger retail and service providers the opportunity to market like-kind properties.

Smart Cities

The evolution of society starts today and change is inevitable. People are changing the way they work, interact between each other and achieve happiness. Companies can reach more people in more places than ever before. The aggregation of people's interaction is monitored through the internet, video cameras and even phone conversations. In order to go "off the grid," you will have to go to an Exuma island with only your sun tan lotion and a hammock hanging under a large palm tree, or to a mountain cabin situated under towering Ponderosa pine trees overlooking a mountain lake. And even then, sophisticated satellites can read your book from outer space.

Columbus, Ohio, just received a "smart city" grant to move it to a tech leader. As the winner of the "Smart City Challenge" in 2016, the Department of Transportation awarded Columbus a $40,000,000 grant to be used to develop next generation transportation with a focus on the user's experience that includes not only the traditional blue-collar professionals, but also entrepreneurs and bankers. Combining car, rail, and bus rapid transit systems on a single grid system monitored through point of contact applications can positively affect the economics of a community. Smart infrastructure systems coupled with private enterprise systems, like Uber, Lyft, Shuddle (safe lifts for children) and Flywheel, provide mobility for the future betterment of a community.

So embrace technology and use it not only for your personal and company goals, but also for the greater good of society. Collecting big data relative to the commuting needs, buying habits, work opportunities and social desires from both the poor and the rich will allow cities to sustain and even grow smarter. Smart cities will provide big data access and transparency to all inhabitants and use their feedback to support government initiatives to enhance lifestyles. The days of work smarter, not longer, are here. Also, the future will require government and business to engage people in informational applications during their expanded social time.

Israel has a reported 5,300 start-up companies, many of which are technology-based. Silicon Valley is the home to multiple pre-IPO $1B start-up companies; Uber, Airbnb and Snapchat are just a few. Israel and Silicon Valley are hubs for immense talent who are reinventing technology and applications that are and will be affecting our everyday lives. Like a well-designed master-planned community, cities and even countries embracing the technology evolution will be at the forefront of the health and well-being of society. Green buildings and even green communities that embrace mass transit, 24-hour lifestyles and work smarter applications will attract the world's talent.

Dubai, the mecca for cultural and business diversity in the Middle East, is undergoing commercial and residential rental rate declines at record levels due to low oil prices. Houston's upscale steak restaurants, for example, have seen a similar precipitous decline in revenue as a result of the same commodity pricing. Attempts to diversify oil-based economies have not insulated real estate in those communities from cyclical oil prices.

Meanwhile, Miami, New York and San Francisco rents and prices continue to escalate to record highs. International buyers enhance local buyer demand and outstrip housing supply. Even at retail pricing levels, above-average appreciation is creating tremendous wealth. The future of communities can continue to be enhanced with technology and the resulting big data that comes from its people can help mold a vibrant economy. Real estate investors active in those communities should be able to achieve above average yields.

Live-work-play communities have been around for centuries. The ability to walk to work from your residence, then walk to a 24-hour fitness facility for an either pre-work, lunch or after-work yoga class, and then go to a fashionable restaurant surrounded by trendy retailers is the ideal lifestyle for some. But given the numerous walkable communities that have incorporated first floor retail with office space and apartments on higher floors, how is someone to select the perfect home?

Do retirees really desire walk-up second and third-floor apartments with a view, or is that the perfect setting for a millennial? Home locations where one can walk to a coffee shop may warrant a different personality than walking to a bar. But how do we "date" a home prior to purchasing a home? With home rental websites like Airbnb, VRBO and Trulia, why would someone buy in an area they are not familiar with prior to experiencing the local lifestyle attributes? Here is an interesting observation:

"Walkable urban regions in the U.S. have a 41 percent higher Gross Domestic Product over non-walkable regions," said Christopher Leinberger, professor at George Washington University School of Business and president of Locus, a national coalition of real estate developers and investors who advocate for sustainable, walkable urban development in metropolitan areas. "That's the difference between countries like Germany and Romania."

Drone delivery systems will help cities and consumers with point of sale timing. Not all cities will embrace drone technology, but those that do will have higher social satisfaction among the population. Drone delivery systems can even help the portion of the population that is not mobile, like the elderly and those recovering from recent accidents. Bringing goods and services to the point of sale will change the way businesses market and interact with their customers. Collecting the data surrounding those consumers is key to successful business growth.

An estimated 9.6 billion people will populate the earth by 2050 and the cities of the future will provide live, work and play environments on both land and sea. Man-made islands like the World and the Palm in Dubai will continue to extend landlocked communities wanting to expand. Big data will be processed every millisecond; water, sewer, food, environment (both inside and outside), social interaction and historical trends along with the then current socio-economic factors will tell businesses and architects what the next years, building environments will look like. Databases will contain every property in the world with actual and digital imagery. Every movement of people in rental and sell/buy real estate will be tracked.

Building downward, into the ground, is reminiscent of centuries old cave dwellers. Temperature control, environmental management and enhanced lighting is providing underground living a viable and inviting opportunity. While technology now allows clear glass office walls to instantly fog up for privacy, future walls will allow for changing sceneries of any landscape on earth, other planets or even the stars. The ability to quickly change the air quality in a contained environment is much more appealing than breathing the air in some of the dirtiest cities in the world. These controlled environments are perfect platforms to process big data and find solutions to enhance lifestyles.

Cities with zero carbon footprints will evolve into some of the most desirable locations to live, work, and play in the world. Underwater and floating homes and hotels are just now entering large-scale spatial opportunities, but as clean water from desalinization and hydroelectric power from tidal and wave movement continues to progress, it makes perfect sense to expand. It is just not oceans, but lakes can provide excellent floating and underwater environments for housing. Big data will allow power generating and battery storage to match usage and transportation options will fit into the home and business, rather than into the garage. Sea farms will provide near-source sustainable food supplies that do not require mass transportation to reach the mouths of healthy millennials.

Big data is forcing architects and designers to change our workspaces. Efficiency is not the primary driver; being connected with technology in a comfortable, almost homey work environment is the key to attracting new talent. Since the 1980s, the average office space per person keeps getting smaller. With increasing rents, employers are looking for work-from-home opportunities, as well as collective work spaces. Even micro-environments within the collective space can cater to a professional's personal preferences – some like it hot, others like it cold. That means heating or cooling does not have to come from air handlers, but can be built into the furniture. They have car seats with environmental controls, why not office chairs.

Sensors and monitors throughout the workspace can digitize the interaction between employees and clients. For a retail store, which at aisles are most popular or most populated, how long does a client stay in one area, where does the client look, does a client pick up a product, and how long do they wait in the check-out line are very important factors retailers need to know. For an office environment, space utilization is key to maximizing revenue; how much of the office needs to be in shared space, how large should conference rooms be and how many are needed? Is a reception area needed? Do professionals really need office phones and hard internet lines? What does the break area look like, and is it a social congregation area or a place where professionals can share ideas, or both?

Should the computers change the look and light intensity of the screen periodically to help employees stay engaged? Are chat programs better than emails for efficiency; should chat programs be in cell phones versus computer apps to enhance walkability at work? If your company is in a "green" certified building, is there anything a company can do internally within the space to find more enhancements?

Big data can measure the spatial needs of its users through engaging professionals in their everyday work environments. The results can then be used to re-engineer the floor plans to enhance productivity and revenue. Now add virtual reality applications to show professionals are the environments and properties they cannot physically touch. The experience is transformational and provides for an enhanced learning environment. The webinar with a camera view can be transformed into a virtual office around the world. Physical restrictions like gravity can be replaced with professionals flying over properties via drone cameras, which can also provide walk through of buildings in cities they have never been to. Overlying heat maps, time sensitive monitoring systems and accelerated time-lapse applications can show what is happening at a property location throughout the day, week, or month.

Real Estate Given Proper Credit

On September 1, 2016 REITs were separated from banks and insurance companies and given their own indices. Equity REITs were reclassified, while mortgage REITs remain in the Financial category. These separate real estate sector will change the Global Industry Classification Standard (GICS). Analysts and investors will be able to isolate the real estate performance of the REIT sector, allowing more clarity, while also asking for enhanced scrutiny and governance. There is no doubt that this will affect REIT pricing and demand, and only time will tell whether it will be positive or negative. Regardless, investors will pay more attention to REIT investments.

SECTOR CLASSIFICATIONS IN GICS
(with Real Estate separated from Financials)

GLOBAL INDUSTRY CLASSIFICATION STANDARD (GICS) 1,500 Companies by "Sector" Classification	MARKET CAPITALIZATION (Billions of dollars)	MARKET CAPITALIZATION (Percent of total)
Information Technology	4,219	19.8
Financials	2,889	13.6
Health Care	2,914	13.7
Consumer Discretionary	2,596	12.2
Industrials	2,340	11.0
Consumer Staples	2,112	9.9
Energy	1,622	7.6
Materials	773	3.6
Real Estate	697	3.2
Utilities	676	3.2
Telecommunication Services	455	2.1

Source: Standard & Poor's and MSCI. Data as of Nov. 30, 2014.

Source: REIT.com

Virtual Reality

When a life insurance company has a $75,000,000 new loan to process, they typically send one person for the site inspection. While that person will do a thorough job, the photographs and notes brought back to the office will not do the property justice. The knowledge gained by all 10 people actually seeing the property would bring a transparency to allow efficiencies in processing.

This is even more important when providing site inspections on international properties. An example was my site inspection of a proposed hotel site on the Guanacaste Peninsula in Costa Rica. A leading hotel destination spa operator flew from Atlanta and was picked up at the airport and transported to a remote jungle location where two locals met us at the property's gravel street front. Expecting a 40-minute hike across the property, we loaded up our water supply while one of the locals draped himself with a flower print, plastic shower curtain. Since I do not speak Spanish and the local did not speak English, we spent the next 40 minutes climbing over fallen trees, walking through creeks with crawfish the size of small lobsters, and ending up on a cliffside with a spectacular view of the Pacific Ocean. Rolling waves crashed against large rock outcroppings and the sun, high in the sky, showcased leatherback turtles swimming like swarms of fish.

The return trip was as eventful; butterflies the size of small plates, and swarms of pink and yellow butterflies floated through the jungle. Before reaching the halfway point, I had to attempt to connect to the shower-curtain-wearing jungle tour guide. I pointed at the shower curtain and asked, "Why shower curtain?" And amazingly his command of the English language came alive, "Bees, Killer Bees, they hate red!" My heart started racing, sweat started falling down my face, and fear raised my adrenalin to an all-time high level as I realized we both were wearing red shirts! After a brief panic attack, I responded, "If we see any bees, you and I are sharing that shower curtain!"

Let's move on to virtual reality, the ability to take 360-degree videos of the property and within minutes allow the team in Omaha, Nebraska, to view the building as if they were there. See and hear the traffic, review the signage (or lack thereof), walk around the building, experience the elevator ride to the top, and stand on the helicopter pad with an aerial view of the surroundings. Better yet, fly a drone off the high-rise and view the building from vantage points not previously available! Get a 360-view of the cooling tower, roof condition, caulking around the exterior windows and even view the subject in relation to the comparable buildings using a headset with camera with a 360-degree virtual reality experience.

Ricoh Theta S for around $350, LG 360 Cam for $300, 360 Fly for $400 and Spericam for $2,500 are various options to start the program. Google Cardboard for as little as $6 with your I-phone can provide your entire due diligence and underwriting team with the ability to experience on "on-site" inspections without ever leaving the office. In the near future, most of the prominent buildings in the world and buildings of massive size (like malls) will have 360-degree walk arounds and through. Big data includes the ability to process interactive media, as well as data points.

Position Yourself for Success

Many millennials are purchasing an URL with their name: www.michaelleraymiller.com. They know that developing a personal brand provides an individuality that differentiates them from their peers. Branding your persona is as important as branding companies. And many, after college, are defecting from the social media that formally monitored their beer drinking successes. Know that your reputation is important and that every astute HR Director will be searching social media to find your "reputation!"

We each have our idea of how we think we are perceived by our friends, family members, and business associates. But if you ask someone else based on your social media, email content, civil duties, voting, and even everyday dress, what is your brand, what would be their response? Ever made a YouTube video? What about a business card for personal branding? Get clear on what your reputation is and better yet, your brand. Then, get the message out!

Live your brand. Do you like wine bars? What about dogs? Volunteer? How about supporting children's welfare? Get some credentials. Real estate agent, certified property manager, MAI and other designations can help you position yourself in this big data world. Continue to build content, every week and every month.

People may start saying better things about you than you say about yourself. What a novel idea. Building a brand talks as much about what you are doing and going to do, as what you did in the past. Positioning yourself in a big data economy requires a proactive approach to your building your brand!

Seven Secrets of Real Estate Millionaires

Many of the great fortunes of our time were made investing in real estate. And you really can get started investing in real estate with little or no money. Simply substitute money with investing time helping other real estate investors find good deals and it always helps to have a real estate license. Starting with Jacob Astor, who had the good fortune to buy much of Manhattan inexpensively, to Sam Zell, who specialized in finding the right time to buy and the right to sell, tens of thousands of great fortunes have been made in real estate. Real estate investing does not require a high level of education or specialized skills to start, but it does require hard work over a period of many years. Following are seven elements common to successful real estate investors.

1. Find a niche in real estate that works for you. It could be investing in houses long term, short term flips of houses, apartments, developing office buildings, or many other options. The most successful people in real estate are specialists. They do not invest in apartments, office, retail, warehouses, land and single-family. There are nuances of location, valuation and operations for each type of property. You will make the rookie mistakes as you learn each new property type, and it will diminish your expertise in a chosen area.

   Management and leasing for apartments, office, retail and warehouses each have factors that are specialized to such property types. Advertising expenses can be substantial for an apartment complex that is not on a major thoroughfare, but minimal for an apartment complex with great signage on a major thoroughfare. A retail center at the intersection of a freeway and a major thoroughfare is different than a mid-block retail center on a major thoroughfare. The layout of the retail center, its orientation to the street and the amount of space in an L-corner configuration all require years of experience to understand. There can be a variety of pitfalls for office buildings such as the parking ratio, whether the existing build-out is consistent with market demand and the plans for major tenants.

The real estate niche you select is less important than developing deep expertise within the investment segment you are desiring to conquer. Consider a variety of options until you find a property type that peaks your interest. There is nothing wrong with changing niches; you may decide the hassle of operating rental houses is not for you. It takes about 10,000 hours, or 5 years of full time work, to become an expert in an area. That's a lot of work and you will make many mistakes along the way (I refer to the mistakes as tuition).

2. Concentrate in one geographic area. Depending on the type of property and your preferences, this could be a neighborhood (for houses), a quadrant in a metro area or a metro area. There is a difference between being a successful apartment investor in your home metro area versus trying to be a successful investor owning apartments in a metro area you do not know well.

    Certainly, there are exceptions; I know of investors who have invested in apartments in California and Texas at the same time, in apartments in Canada and Texas concurrently, and in land in many metro areas across the Sunbelt. Just know that there are nuances in real estate submarkets which are difficult to discern. Likewise, there are properties which have not performed well for many years for a variety of reasons. In your home market, you will have seen these properties and understand the pitfalls. In a new market, you will have to climb a long and steep learning curve for a metro area you do not know well.

    Thirty years ago I was told that it takes 10 good deals to make up for one bad deal. In general, I have found it to be true. Of course, it depends on the cost of the bad deal. You are much more likely to make a bad deal in a market you do not understand.

The market you select does not have to be your home market. If you live in Iowa, you may decide the appreciation will be greater in Florida, Texas, or California. However, if you select a market not familiar to you, there will need to be a large investment of time to understand the metro area you are selecting. Ideally, you would move to the market to be able to spend as much time as possible familiarizing yourself with it.

Stocks and bonds are fungible. One share of Exxon is exactly the same as another share of Exxon. Real estate is not fungible. The financial and emotional pain of purchasing a property which requires a substantial investment of cash is intense. It can take years to resolve a bad deal, particularly if there are management problems associated with physical condition, undesirable tenants, or low occupancy. Your risk of a bad deal will increase exponentially if you invest in an area you do not know well.

3. Don't pay more taxes than necessary. This includes property taxes, income taxes, 1031 exchanges, and estate taxes. The government is akin to a lender that is never satisfied and never fully paid.

Property taxes are rent you pay to the government to keep your property. The government demands property taxes whether you are making money or not. In effect, the government has a first lien on the property, and they want to be paid annually. Most property taxes are ad valorem, or based on value. The property taxes are based on the assessed value, typically established by an appraiser working for the county assessor's office, for the property times the tax rate established by local government, school districts, or bonding jurisdictions. You can impact the property taxes by appealing the assessed value, depending on the location. It is almost impossible to impact the tax rate.

Appeal property taxes annually or as often as makes sense. In some states, such as California, the taxable value is so low compared to market value that appealing does not make sense. Conversely, in Texas many appraisal districts revalue property tax assessments annually.

4. Income tax planning is a complicated issue and beyond the scope of this discussion. If you are an active real estate investor, you can deduct losses from real estate against other ordinary income. There is a gray area regarding which operating expenses are capital expenses and which can be deducted as expenses. This area is as much art as science. Many real estate investments do not generate much ordinary income during the ownership period due to the cost of interest, depreciation, and operating expenses. The net effect of real estate investment can be to convert ordinary income to capital gains income.

Many real estate investors use 1031 exchanges to avoid paying capital gains taxes when they sell real estate. While this can be an excellent tool, I have seen many investors select a poor investment as the replacement property to avoid paying taxes. In many cases, it can be better to pay the capital gains tax and keep the remainder of the cash.

5. Use cost segregation to increase depreciation and to reduce and defer income taxes. Cost segregation allows accelerated depreciation at the initial years following the acquisition, increasing the return on the investment.

6. Develop a deep level of expertise in the property type where you specialize. Buying, operating and selling real estate is nothing like buying marketable securities such as stocks and bonds.

7. Serious money in real estate is made by either buying at a discount or by choosing an area which will experience above-average appreciation in value. The latter requires investors to hold the real estate asset for some time.

Market timing is easier in real estate than in the stock market. Data is available regarding property under construction, proposed construction, absorption of existing vacant inventory, vacancy rates and rental rates. There is a cycle to real estate markets which is well understood and documented.

Conclusion

Predicting and communicating future trends can most effectively be done by processing big data. Not only businesses, but also communities can benefit from well-managed communication of trends and their affect. We are at a point in time where rapid change will affect how we do our work. Businesses who know how to extract the trends, client habits and future opportunities of their environment will lead. Investment opportunities will be tracked with increased clarity, as research will have less human subjectivity and increased background analysis. The tools currently used by the leading investment banks, Wall Street firms and multi-national corporations will be available to on a desktop in Des Moines, Iowa.

Like dating websites, where you should live based on your career, lifestyle, hobbies and relationship goals will be factored into search engines. Quality over quantity will be the goal of many. Time management to reach that goal will require each of us to focus on what is important. For those outward looking individuals who have social or even government initiatives, they will use solutions found from big data in making the greatest presence with the least effort. Each day, a person can make decisions on how they can change their own future and their family's future through on-line education, networking and work opportunities. Talented professionals can work a full-time job and use a few precious hours after work to contract their programming, data entry, phone proficiency, and various talents to companies and others around the world at per hour pay rates many times higher than their primary work. Those talents can be aggregated with others to deliver services and products that previously took large employment pools working in a single building environment.

As we cannot predict exactly what the future holds, because of quickly evolving technologies, we know the way we interact socially and within business environments will be much different in the future. We live at a time where we can create a business in minutes (in 10 minutes we purchased 6 domain names for $18), and take it internationally in hours. The ability to drive more customers to your website than could ever visit a store and your ability to reach clients who need your help to solve business problems are the only things standing in the way of success! It is a lot more exciting working on your terms than those dictated by a large company where you never had any say-so on how best to do your job.

Are you ready to participate in the new economy as an entrepreneur? I-tunes has over 1.2 million apps. Over 100 billion downloads have occurred. Do not accept the status-quo, look for a new solution. Schedule a time to build your solution to a problem, create a solution that is an interactive experience, make sure it shows well on a smart phone, use big data to process the solution like no one before has been able to and get it into the internet so the business solution can scale. If you do not do it, someone else will.

Do not turn your back on the inevitable; change is at hand and you can be a solution, or a subscriber. Good luck!

www.BigDataMillionaire.com